POX AMERICANA
Exposing the American Empire

POX AMERICANA
Exposing the American Empire

Edited by
John Bellamy Foster
Robert W. McChesney

POX AMERICANA
John Bellamy Foster and Robert W. McChesney (Eds.)

Published in agreement with Monthly Review Press, New York
for publication and sale only in the Indian Subcontinent
(India, Pakistan, Bangladesh, Nepal, Maldives,
Bhutan & Sri Lanka)

First Published in India, 2006

ISBN 81-87879-77-7 (Hb)

Published by
AAKAR BOOKS
28 E Pocket IV, Mayur Vihar Phase I, Delhi-110 091
Phone : 011-2279 5505 Telefax : 011-2279 5641
aakarbooks@bol.net.in; www.aakarbooks.com

Printed at
Mudrak, 30 A, Patparganj, Delhi-110 091

Contents

PART THREE: Resistance

PREFACE

JOHN BELLAMY FOSTER
and ROBERT W. MCCHESNEY

On June 10, 1963, President John F. Kennedy delivered a Commencement Address at American University in Washington, D.C., in which he declared that the peace that the United States sought was "not a Pax Americana enforced on the world by American weapons of war." His remarks were a response to criticisms of the United States advanced in a recently published Soviet text on *Military Strategy*. Kennedy dismissed the charge that "American imperialist circles" were "preparing to unleash different kinds of wars" including "preventative war." The Soviet text, he pointed out, had stated, "The political aims of American imperialists were and still are to enslave economically and politically the European and other capitalist countries and, after the latter are transformed into obedient tools, to unify them in various military-political blocs and groups directed against the socialist countries. The main aim of all this is to achieve world domination." In Kennedy's words, these were "wholly baseless and incredible claims," the work of Marxist "propagandists." "The United States, as the world knows, will never start a war."[1]

Despite such high level denials, the notion of a "Pax Americana" enforced by American arms was to become the preferred designation for those attempting to justify what was portrayed as a benevolent American Empire. Thus in his widely read book *Pax Americana*, first published in 1967 during the Vietnam War, Ronald Steel wrote of "the benevolent imperialism of Pax Americana" characterized by "empire-building for noble ends rather than for such base motives as profit and influence." A chapter of Steel's book on foreign aid as an "element of imperialism" was entitled "The White Man's Burden," hearkening back to Rudyard Kipling's celebrated poem calling on the United States to exercise an imperialist role in the Philippines following the Spanish-American War of 1898.[2] Such explicit imperial views, largely suppressed in the United States after the U.S. defeat in Vietnam, have now resurfaced in a post-Cold War world marked by U.S. wars in Afghanistan and Iraq and by a permanent U.S.-led "War on Terrorism." Once again we hear establishment calls for the "defense of Pax Americana" and even renewals of the old cry to take up "the White Man's burden."

Kennedy had depicted the global military expansion of the United States as an attempt to contain Communism. Today the Cold War is over. The Soviet Union is no more. Yet at the beginning of the twenty-first century the United States is viewed more than ever by the world population as an imperialist power, enforcing its will unilaterally by force of arms. Since the fall of the Soviet Union we have seen the largest military interventions by the United States in Europe since the Second World War. The U.S. war machine has waged full-scale conventional wars in the Middle East. The United States now has military bases in locales such as Central Asia that were previously beyond the reach of the American Empire. In the 2003 invasion of Iraq, Washington made it clear that it was conducting a preventive war in light of the potential threat represented by weapons of mass destruction that could be used against the United States. The fact that there was no evidence of the existence of such weapons prior to the war did not seem to matter because a declaration by the administration that such weapons existed was deemed sufficient. Nor did it seem to matter after the war that no such weapons were found since once the invasion had taken place the new reality on the ground in Iraq dictated all. In this way imperialism provided its own justification.

Rather than break with earlier U.S. history these recent military actions represent the continuation and acceleration of an old pattern—going back to the second half of the 1940s (and further back in U.S. history). Major U.S. interventions, both overt and covert, include: China (1945), Greece (1947–49), Korea (1950–53), Iran (1953), Guatemala (1954), Indochina (1954–73), Lebanon (1958), the Congo (1960–64), Cuba (1961), Indonesia (1965), the Dominican Republic (1965–66), Chile (1973), Angola (1976–92), Lebanon (1982–84), Grenada (1983–84), Afghanistan (1979–1989), El Salvador (1981–92), Nicaragua (1981–90), Panama (1989–90), Iraq (1991), Somalia (1992–94), Haiti (1994), Bosnia (1995), Yugoslavia (1999), Afghanistan (2001—), and Iraq (2003—). The enormous scale of U.S. military engagement is evident in the fact that its military bases gird the globe. Chalmers Johnson has written in his *Sorrows of Empire*, "As distinct from other peoples on this earth, most Americans do not recognize—or do not choose to recognize—that the United States dominates the world through its military power. Due to government secrecy, they are often ignorant of the fact that their government garrisons the globe. They do not realize that a vast network of American military bases on every continent but Antarctica actually constitutes a new form of empire."[3]

The primary goals of U.S. imperialism have always been to open up investment opportunities to U.S. corporations and to allow such corporations to gain preferential access to crucial natural resources. Inasmuch as such expansion promotes U.S. hegemony it tends to increase the international competitiveness of U.S. firms and the profits they enjoy. At the same time U.S. imperialism promotes the interests of the other core states and of capitalism as a whole insofar as these are in accord with U.S. requirements. Such goals, however, frequently put the United States in conflict with other imperial states since an empire by definition is a sphere of exploitation in which a single imperial power plays the dominant role. Moreover, the logic of empire militates against all attempts to change the status quo in the periphery of the system—if not in the center as well.

For these reasons militarism and imperialism are inseparable for U.S. capitalism, as they are for capitalism as a whole. Although spending almost as much on the military as all other states combined, the United States finds itself constantly in need of more armaments, more new weapons systems, more soldiers, etc. As it relies increasingly on the military to maintain and where necessary restore its economic and political hegemony on a global scale the problem of imperial overstretch becomes chronic and insurmountable.

By the end of the Vietnam War the mask had been torn off the American Empire. In 1970 Steel issued a revised edition of *Pax Americana* with a new final chapter entitled "No More Vietnams?" The main thrust of this new chapter, written in a period marked by the looming U.S. defeat in Vietnam, was entirely opposed to the chapters that preceded it. "After Vietnam, the Dominican Republic, and the Greek junta," Steel wrote, "it is not so easy for an American President to speak with a straight face of the nation's foreign policy being based on the 'liberation of man' or the 'survival of liberty.'"[4] Pax Americana was revealed as imperialism pure and simple.

Nonetheless, the American Imperium did not fade away with this loss of "face." The momentum behind such imperialism remained. Washington held on to its empire awaiting new opportunities for expansion. The empire struck back in the late 1970s and 80s under Carter and Reagan. The rapid decline and fall of the Soviet Union at the beginning of the 1990s opened up the way to a full scale U.S. military intervention in the Middle East for the first time, with the onset of the 1991 Gulf War between the United States and Iraq. No longer simply intervening against revolutionary movements, the United States, now the sole superpower, gave notice to the world that a substantial departure from the global status quo in any direction would be met with overwhelming force. Noting this, Harry Magdoff and Paul Sweezy wrote in a July–August 1991 article entitled "Pox Americana":

> The United States, it seems, has locked itself into a course with the gravest implications for the whole world. Change is the only certain law of the universe. It cannot be stopped. If societies are prevented from trying to solve their problems in their own ways, they will certainly not solve them in ways dictated by others. And if they cannot move forward, they will inevitably move backward. This is what is happening in a large part of the world today, and the United States, the most powerful nation with unlimited means of coercion at its disposal, seems to be telling the others that this is a fate that must be accepted on pain of violent destruction.[5]

With the current death toll of both the Iraqi population and U.S. soldiers rising in Iraq during still another war and occupation, with the atrocities and torture inflicted by the United States in Abu Ghraib prison and elsewhere leading to protests across the globe, with the barbarism of the U.S. intervention in Iraq in all of its aspects increasingly evident, it is more difficult than ever to maintain the illusion of the "benevolent imperialism of Pax Americana." The American Empire has truly become a *Pox* Americana in the eyes of the world, and exposure of its inner workings has become an urgent necessity. If the United States seems bent, as Magdoff and Sweezy suggested more than a decade ago, on playing "Samson in the temple of humanity" at least now there is a growing world awareness of that fact. It is the purpose of this book to deepen this critical understanding in ways that will help equip humanity for the major anti-imperialist struggles that lie ahead.

Most of the essays in this volume were prepared for the "Imperialism Today" conference held in Burlington, Vermont, on May 3, 2003, and published in a July–August 2003 special issue of *Monthly Review* in honor of Harry Magdoff's ninetieth birthday. Two of the pieces, Noam Chomsky's "Imperialist Ambition" and John Bellamy Foster, Harry Magdoff and Robert W. McChesney's "Kipling, 'The White Man's Burden,' and U.S. Imperialism" appeared in other issues of *Monthly Review*, in May 2003 and November 2003, respectively. Michael Yates assisted in the editing of both the special issue and the present book. We dedicate this book to Harry Magdoff and to the memory of Paul Sweezy.

May 22, 2004

PART ONE

U.S. Imperialism Has a Long History

Today in Afghanistan, Iraq, and elsewhere, the United States is engaging in what even conventional analysts are calling "imperialism." For a long time, the word *imperialism* was outside the realm of respectable scholarly discourse, used only by those whom respectable scholars would label "the far left." Of course, now that the term is current again, most contemporary scholars use it in a positive way, implying that the United States although playing an imperial role is not at all like former imperialist powers. The United States practices a benign imperialism, they say, one aimed not at securing monopoly control of the world's resources or assisting U.S. corporations to accumulate capital through domination of the globe but at helping other nations to achieve independence and democracy.

Nothing could be further from the truth, as the essays in this section make abundantly clear. The United States has a long and inglorious history of imperialism, going back to the very beginning of the republic. And this imperialism has roots in even earlier periods. There is a continuity of ideas and action from the time of the Spanish defeat of the Muslims in the fifteenth century and the extermination of Indians in the "New World" from the time of Columbus onward, to the conquest of Iraq today.

It is important to understand this history of imperialism and especially U.S. imperialism. Doing so keeps us from embracing notions such as *rogue regimes* and myths that the United States was once a non-imperialist nation. It helps us to understand that imperialism has, from the beginning, been part and parcel of capitalism and will not be eliminated until capitalism itself is ended.

1

Kipling, the "White Man's Burden," and U.S. Imperialism

JOHN BELLAMY FOSTER, HARRY MAGDOFF,
AND ROBERT W. MCCHESNEY

We are living in a period in which the rhetoric of empire knows few bounds. In a special report on "America and Empire" in August 2003, the London-based *Economist* magazine asked whether the United States would, in the event of "regime changes . . . effected peacefully" in Iran and Syria, "really be prepared to shoulder the white man's burden across the Middle East?" The answer it gave was that this was "unlikely"—the U.S. commitment to empire did not go so far. What is significant, however, is that the question was asked at all.[1]

Current U.S. wars in Afghanistan and Iraq have led observers to wonder whether there aren't similarities and historical linkages between the "new" imperialism of the twenty-first century and the imperialism of the nineteenth and early twentieth centuries. As Jonathan Marcus, the BBC's defense correspondent, commented in July 2003:

> It should be remembered that more than one hundred years ago, the British poet Rudyard Kipling wrote his famous poem about what he styled as "the white man's burden"—a warning about the responsibilities of empire that was directed not at London but at Washington and its new- found imperial responsibilities in the Philippines. It is not clear if President George W. Bush is a reader of poetry or of Kipling. But Kipling's sentiments are as relevant today as they were when the poem was written in the aftermath of the Spanish-American War.[2]

A number of other modern-day proponents of imperialism have also drawn connections with Kipling's poem, which begins with the lines:

Take up the White Man's burden—
Send forth the best ye breed—

Before discussing the reasons for this sudden renewed interest in Kipling's "White Man's Burden," it is necessary to provide some background on the history of U.S. imperialism to put the poem in context.

FROM THE SPANISH-AMERICAN WAR TO THE PHILIPPINE-AMERICAN WAR

In the Spanish-American War of 1898 the United States seized the Spanish colonies in the Caribbean and the Pacific, emerging for the first time as a world power.[3] As in Cuba, Spanish colonial rule in the Philippines had given rise to a national liberation struggle. Immediately after the U.S. naval bombardment of Manila on May 1, 1898, in which the Spanish fleet was destroyed, Admiral Dewey sent a gunboat to fetch the exiled Filipino revolutionary leader Emilio Aguinaldo from Hong Kong. The United States wanted Aguinaldo to lead a renewed revolt against Spain to prosecute the war before U.S. troops could arrive. The Filipinos were so successful that in less than two months they had all but defeated the Spanish on the main island of Luzon, bottling up the remaining Spanish troops in the capital city of Manila, while almost all of the archipelago fell into Filipino hands. In June, Filipino leaders issued their own Declaration of Independence, based on the U.S. model. When U.S. forces finally arrived at the end of June, the fifteen thousand Spanish troops holed up in Manila were surrounded by the Filipino army entrenched around the city—so that U.S. forces had to request permission to cross Filipino lines to engage these remaining Spanish troops. The Spanish army surrendered Manila to U.S. forces after only a few hours of fighting on August 13, 1898. In an agreement between the United States and Spain, Filipino forces were kept out of the city and were allowed no part in the surrender. This was the final battle of the war. John Hay, U.S. ambassador to Britain, captured the imperialist spirit of the time when he wrote that the Spanish-American War as a whole was "a splendid little war."

With the fighting against Spain over, however, the United States refused to acknowledge the existence of the new Philippine Republic. In October 1898 the McKinley administration publicly revealed for the first time that it intended to annex the entire Philippines. In arriving at this decision President McKinley is reported to have said that "God Almighty" had ordered him to make the

Philippines a U.S. colony. Within days of this announcement the New England Anti-Imperialist League was established in Boston. Its membership was to include such luminaries as Mark Twain, William James, Charles Francis Adams, and Andrew Carnegie. Nevertheless, the administration went ahead and concluded the Treaty of Paris in December, in which Spain agreed to cede the Philippines, along with its other possessions seized by the United States, to the new imperial power.

This was followed by a fierce debate in the Senate on the ratification of the treaty, centering on the status of the Philippines, which, except for the city of Manila, was under the control of the nascent Philippine Republic. On February 4, 1899, U.S. troops, under orders to provoke a conflict with the Filipino forces ringing Manila, were moved into disputed ground lying between U.S. and Filipino lines on the outskirts of the city. When they encountered Filipino soldiers, the U.S. soldiers called "Halt" and then opened fire, killing three. The U.S. forces immediately began a general offensive with their full firepower in what amounted to a surprise attack (the top Filipino officers were then away attending a lavish celebratory ball), inflicting enormous casualties on the Filipino troops. The *San Francisco Call* reported on February 5 that the moment the news reached Washington, McKinley told "an intimate friend . . . that the Manila engagement would, in his opinion, insure the ratification of the treaty tomorrow."

These calculations proved correct. The following day the Senate ratified the Treaty of Paris officially ending the Spanish-American War. Under the treaty Spain ceded Guam, Puerto Rico, and the Philippines to the United States, and Cuba came under U.S. control. It stipulated that the United States would pay Spain $20 million for the territories that it gained through the war. But this did little to disguise the fact that the Spanish-American War was an outright seizure of an overseas colonial empire by the United States, in response to the perceived need of U.S. business, just recovering from an economic downturn, for new global markets.

The United States immediately pushed forward in the Philippine-American War that it had begun two days before—in what was to prove to be one of history's more barbaric wars of imperial conquest. The U.S. goal in this period was to expand not only into the Caribbean but also far into the Pacific—and by colonizing the Philippine Islands, to gain a doorway into the huge Chinese market. (In 1900 the United States sent troops from the Philippines to China to join with the other imperial powers in putting down the Boxer Rebellion.) Kipling's "White Man's Burden," subtitled "The United States and the Philippine Islands," was published in *McClure's Magazine* in

February 1899.[4] It was written when the debate over ratification of the Treaty of Paris was still taking place, and while the anti-imperialist movement in the United States was loudly decrying the plan to annex the Philippines. Kipling urged the United States, with special reference to the Philippines, to join Britain in the pursuit of the racial responsibilities of empire:

> Your new-caught sullen peoples,
> Half devil and half child.

Many in the United States, including President McKinley and Theodore Roosevelt, welcomed Kipling's rousing call for the United States to engage in "savage wars," beginning in the Philippines. Senator Albert J. Beveridge of Indiana declared: "God has not been preparing the English-speaking and Teutonic peoples for a thousand years for nothing but vain and idle self-contemplation and self-admiration. . . . He has made us adept in government that we may administer government among savage and senile peoples." In the end, more than 126,000 officers and men were sent to the Philippines to put down the Filipino resistance during a war that lasted officially from 1899 to 1902 but actually continued much longer, with sporadic resistance continuing for most of a decade. U.S. troops logged 2,800 engagements with the Filipino resistance. At least a quarter of a million Filipinos, most of them civilians, were killed along with 4,200 U.S. soldiers (more than ten times the number of U.S. fatalities in the Spanish–American War).[5]

From the beginning it was clear that the Filipino forces were unable to match the United States in conventional warfare. They therefore quickly switched to guerrilla warfare. U.S. troops boasted in a popular marching song that they would "civilize them with the Krag" (referring to the Norwegian-designed gun with which the U.S. forces were outfitted). Yet they found themselves facing interminable small attacks and ambushes by Filipinos, who often carried long knives known as bolos. These guerrilla attacks resulted in combat deaths of U.S. soldiers in small numbers on a regular basis. As in all prolonged guerrilla wars, the strength of the Filipino resistance was due to the fact that it had the support of the Filipino population. As General Arthur MacArthur (the father of Douglas MacArthur), who became military governor of the Philippines in 1900, confided to a reporter in 1899:

> When I first started in against these rebels, I believed that Aguinaldo's troops represented only a faction. I did not like to believe that the whole population of Luzon—the native population that is—was opposed to us and our offers of aid and good

> government. But after having come this far, after having occupied several towns and cities in succession. . . I have been reluctantly compelled to believe that the Filipino masses are loyal to Aguinaldo and the government which he heads.

Faced with a guerrilla struggle supported by the vast majority of the population, the U.S. military responded by resettling populations in concentration camps, burning down villages (Filipinos were sometimes forced to carry the petrol used to burn down their own homes), and engaging in mass hangings and bayonetings of suspects, systematic rape of women and girls, and torture. The most infamous torture technique, used repeatedly in the war, was the so-called water cure. Vast quantities of water were forced down the throats of prisoners. Their stomachs were then stepped on so that the water shot out three feet in the air "like an artesian well." Most victims died not long afterwards. General Frederick Funston did not hesitate to announce that he had personally strung up a group of thirty-five Filipino civilians suspected of supporting the revolutionaries. Major Edwin Glenn saw no reason to deny the charge that he had made a group of forty-seven Filipino prisoners kneel and "repent of their sins" before bayoneting and clubbing them to death. General Jacob Smith ordered his troops to "kill and burn," to target "everything over ten," and to turn the island of Samar into "a howling wilderness." General William Shafter in California declared that it might be necessary to kill half the Filipino population to bring "perfect justice" to the other half. During the Philippine War the United States reversed the normal casualty statistics of war—usually many more are wounded than killed. According to official statistics (discussed in Congressional hearings on the war) U.S. troops killed fifteen times as many Filipinos as they wounded. This fit with frequent reports by U.S. soldiers that wounded and captured Filipino combatants were summarily executed.

The war continued after the capture of Aguinaldo in March 1901 but was declared officially over by President Theodore Roosevelt on July 4, 1902—in an attempt to quell criticism of U.S. atrocities. At that time, the northern islands had been mostly "pacified" but the conquest of the southern islands was still ongoing and the struggle continued for years—though the United States from then on characterized the rebels as mere bandits.

In the southern Philippines the U.S. colonial army was at war with Muslim Filipinos, known as Moros. In 1906 what came to be known as the Moro Massacre was carried out by U.S. troops when at least nine hundred Filipinos, including women and children, were trapped in a volcanic crater on the island of Jolo and shot at and bombarded for days. All of the Filipinos were killed while the U.S. troops suffered only a handful of casualties. Mark

Twain responded to early reports (which indicated that those massacred totaled six hundred rather than nine hundred men, women, and children, as later determined) with bitter satire: "With six hundred engaged on each side, we lost fifteen men killed outright, and we had thirty-two wounded—counting that nose and that elbow. The enemy numbered six hundred—including women and children—and we abolished them utterly, leaving not even a baby alive to cry for its dead mother. *This is incomparably the greatest victory that was ever achieved by the Christian soldiers of the United States.*" Viewing a widely distributed photo that showed U.S. soldiers overlooking piles of Filipino dead in the crater, W. E. B. Du Bois declared in a letter to Moorfield Storey, president of the Anti- Imperialist League (and later first president of the NAACP), that it was "the most illuminating thing I have ever seen. I want especially to have it framed and put upon the walls of my recitation room to impress upon the students what wars and especially Wars of Conquest really mean."[6]

President Theodore Roosevelt immediately commended his good friend General Leonard Wood, who had carried out the Moro Massacre, writing: "I congratulate you and the officers and men of your command upon the brilliant feat of arms wherein you and they so well upheld the honor of the American flag." Like Kipling, Roosevelt seldom hesitated to promote the imperialist cause or to forward doctrines of racial superiority. Yet Kipling's novels, stories, and verses were distinguished by the fact that they seemed to many individuals in the white world to evoke a transcendent and noble cause. At the same time, they did not fail to reach out and acknowledge the hatred that the colonized had for the colonizer. In presenting the Nobel Prize in Literature to Kipling in 1907, the Nobel Committee proclaimed, "His imperialism is not of the uncompromising type that pays no regard to the sentiments of others."[7] It was precisely this that made Kipling's "White Man's Burden" and other outpourings from his pen so effective as ideological veils for a barbaric reality.

The year Kipling's poem appeared, 1899, marked not only the end of the Spanish- American War (through the ratification of the Treaty of Paris) and the beginning of the Philippine-American War, but also the beginning of the Boer War in South Africa. These were classic imperialist wars, and they generated anti-imperialist movements and radical critiques in response. It was the Boer War that gave rise to John A. Hobson's *Imperialism, A Study* (1902), which argued, "Nowhere under such conditions"—referring specifically to British imperialism in South Africa—"is the theory of white government as a trust for civilization made valid." The opening sentence of Lenin's *Imperialism, the Highest Stage of Capitalism*, written in 1915, stated that "especially since the

Spanish- American War (1898), and the Anglo-Boer War (1899–1902), the economic and also the political literature of the two hemispheres has more and more often adopted the term 'imperialism' in order to define the present era."

KIPLING'S MESSAGE TO IMPERIALISTS AFTER ONE HUNDRED YEARS

Although imperialism has remained a reality over the last century, the term itself was branded as beyond the pale within polite establishment circles for most of the twentieth century—so great was the anti-imperialist outrage arising from the Philippine–American War and the Boer War, and so effective was the Marxist theory of imperialism in stripping the veil away from global capitalist relations. In the last few years, however, "imperialism" has once again become a rallying cry—for neoconservatives and neoliberals alike. As Alan Murray, Washington bureau chief of CNBC recently acknowledged in a statement directed principally at the elites, "We are all, it seems, imperialists now."[8]

If one were to doubt for a moment that the current expansion of U.S. empire is but the continuation of a century-long history of U.S. overseas imperialism, Michael Ignatieff, professor of human rights policy at Harvard's Kennedy School of Government, has made it as clear as day:

> The Iraq operation most resembles the conquest of the Philippines between 1898 and 1902. Both were wars of conquest, both were urged by an ideological elite on a divided country and both cost much more than anyone had bargained for. Just as in Iraq, winning the war was the easy part. . . . More than 120,000 American troops were sent to the Philippines to put down the guerrilla resistance, and 4,000 never came home. It remains to be seen whether Iraq will cost thousands of American lives—and whether the American public will accept such a heavy toll as the price of success in Iraq.[9]

With representatives of the establishment openly espousing imperialist ambitions, we shouldn't be surprised at the repeated attempts to bring back the "white man's burden" argument in one form or another. In the closing pages of his prize-winning book, *The Savage Wars of Peace*,[10] Max Boot quotes Kipling's poem:

> Take up the White Man's burden—
>   And reap his old reward:

The blame of those ye better,
The hate of those ye guard—

Boot insists that Kipling was right, that "colonists everywhere, usually received scant thanks afterward." Nevertheless, we should be encouraged, he tells us, by the fact that "the bulk of the people did not resist American occupation, as they surely would have done if it had been nasty and brutal. Many Cubans, Haitians, Dominicans, and others may secretly have welcomed U.S. rule." Boot's main implication seems clear enough—the United States should again take up the "white man's burden." His book, published in 2002, ends by arguing that the United States should have deposed Saddam Hussein and occupied Iraq at the time of the 1991 Gulf War. That task, he implied, remained to be accomplished.

Boot is former editorial features editor of the *Wall Street Journal,* now Olin Senior Fellow in National Security Studies with the Council on Foreign Relations. The title of *The Savage Wars of Peace* was taken straight from a line in Kipling's "White Man's Burden." Boot's 428-page glorification of U.S. imperialist wars received the Best Book of 2002 Award from the *Washington Post*, *Christian Science Monitor*, and the *Los Angeles Times* and won the 2003 General Wallace M. Greene Jr. Award for the best nonfiction book pertaining to Marine Corps history. Boot contends that the Philippine War was "one of the most successful counterinsurgencies waged by a Western army in modern times" and declares that "by the standards of the day, the conduct of U.S. soldiers was better than average for colonial wars." The U.S. imperial role in the Philippines, the subject of Kipling's "White Man's Burden," is thus being presented as a model for the kind of imperial role that Boot and other neoconservatives are now urging on the United States. Even before the war in Iraq, Ignatieff remarked: "Imperialism used to be the white man's burden. This gave it a bad reputation. But imperialism doesn't stop being necessary because it is politically incorrect"—a point that might well be read as extending to the "white man's burden" itself.[11]

The Philippine-American War is now being rediscovered as the closest approximation in U.S. history to the problems the United States is encountering in Iraq. Further, the United States has taken advantage of the September 11, 2001 attacks to intervene militarily not just in the Middle East but also around the globe—including in the Philippines, where it has deployed thousands of troops to aid the Philippine army in fighting Moro insurgents in the southern islands. In this new imperialist climate Niall Ferguson, Herzog Professor of History at the Stern School of Business, New York

University, and one of the principal advocates of the new imperialism, has addressed Kipling's poem "The White Man's Burden" in his book *Empire*.[12] "No one," Ferguson tells us,

> would dare use such politically incorrect language today. The reality is nevertheless that the United States has—whether it admits it or not— taken up some kind of global burden, just as Kipling urged. It considers itself responsible not just for waging a war against terrorism and rogue states, but also for spreading the benefits of capitalism and democracy overseas. And just like the British Empire before it, the American Empire unfailingly acts in the name of liberty, even when its own self-interest is manifestly uppermost.

Despite Ferguson's claim that "no one would dare" to call this "the white man's burden" today since it is "politically incorrect," sympathetic references to the term keep cropping up—and in the most privileged circles. Boot—hardly a marginal figure, since affiliated with the influential Council on Foreign Relations—is a good example. Like Ferguson, he tries to incorporate the "white man's burden" into a long history of idealistic intervention, downplaying the realities of racism and imperialism: "In the early twentieth century," he writes in his book's final chapter (entitled "In Defense of the Pax Americana"), "Americans talked of spreading Anglo-Saxon civilization and taking up the 'white man's burden'; today they talk of spreading democracy and defending human rights. Whatever you call it, this represents an idealistic impulse that has always been a big part in America's impetus for going to war."

Today's imperialists see Kipling's poem mainly as an attempt to stiffen the spine of the U.S. ruling class of his day in preparation for what he called "the savage wars of peace." And it is precisely in this way that they now allude to the "white man's burden" in relation to the twenty-first century. Thus for the *Economist* magazine the question is simply whether the United States is "prepared to shoulder the white man's burden across the Middle East."

As an analyst of, as well as a spokesman for, imperialism, Kipling was head and shoulders above this, in the sense that he accurately perceived the looming contradictions of his own time. He knew that the British Empire was overstretched and doomed—even as he struggled to redeem it and to inspire the rising United States to enter the imperial stage alongside it. Only two years before writing "The White Man's Burden" he wrote his celebrated verse "Recessional":

> Far-called, our navies melt away;
> 	On dune and headland sinks the fire;
> Lo, all our pomp of yesterday

Is one with Nineveh and Tyre!
Judge of Nations, spare us yet,
Lest we forget—lest we forget!

The United States is now leading the way into a new phase of imperialism. This will be marked not only by increased conflict between center and periphery—rationalized in the West by veiled and not-so-veiled racism—but also by increased intercapitalist rivalry. This will likely speed up the long-run decline of the American Empire, rather than the reverse. And in this situation a call for a closing of the ranks between those of European extraction (Samuel Huntington's "clash of civilizations" argument or some substitute) is likely to become more appealing among U.S. and British elites. It should be remembered that Kipling's "White Man's Burden" was a call for the joint exploitation of the globe by what Du Bois was later to call "the white masters of the world" in the face of the ebbing of British fortunes.[13] At no time, then, should we underestimate the three-fold threat of militarism, imperialism, and racism—or forget that capitalist societies have historically been identified with all three.

2

Imperial Ambition

NOAM CHOMSKY, *interviewed by* DAVID BARSAMIAN
(March 22, 2003)

DAVID BARSAMIAN: What are the regional implications of the U.S. invasion and occupation of Iraq?

NOAM CHOMSKY: I think not only the region but the world in general perceives it correctly as a kind of easy test case to try to establish a norm for use of military force, which was declared in general terms last September. Last September, *The National Security Strategy of the United States of America* was issued. It presented a somewhat novel and unusually extreme doctrine on the use of force in the world. And it's hard not to notice that the drumbeat for war in Iraq coincided with that. It also coincided with the onset of the congressional campaign. All these are tied together.

The new doctrine was not one of preemptive war, which arguably falls within some stretching of the United Nations Charter, but rather of something that doesn't even begin to have any grounds in international law, namely, preventive war. The doctrine, you recall, was that the United States would rule the world by force, and that if there is any challenge perceived to its domination, a challenge perceived in the distance, invented, imagined, whatever, then the U.S. will have the right to destroy that challenge before it becomes a threat. That's preventive war, not preemptive war.

And if you want to declare a doctrine, a powerful state has the capacity to create what is called a new norm. So if India invades Pakistan to put an end to monstrous atrocities, that's not a norm. But if the United States bombs Serbia on dubious grounds, that's a norm. That's what power means.

So if you want to establish a new norm, you have to do something. And the easiest way to do it is to select a completely defenseless target, which can be completely overwhelmed by the most massive military force in human history. However, in order to do that credibly, at least to your own population, you have to frighten them. So the defenseless target has to be turned into an awesome threat to survival which was responsible for September 11 and is about to attack us again, and so on and so forth. And that was indeed done. Beginning last September, there was a massive effort which substantially succeeded in convincing Americans, alone in the world, that Saddam Hussein is not only a monster but a threat to their existence. That was the content of the October congressional resolution and a lot of things since. And it shows in the polls. And by now about half the population even believes that he was responsible for September 11.

So all this falls together. You have the doctrine pronounced. You have a norm established in a very easy case. The population is driven into a panic and, alone in the world, believes fantasies of this kind and therefore is willing to support military force in self-defense. And if you believe this, then it really is self-defense. So it's kind of like a textbook example of aggression, with the purpose of extending the scope of further aggression. Once the easy case is handled, you can move on to think of harder cases.

Those are the main reasons why so much of the world is overwhelmingly opposed to the war. It's not just the attack on Iraq. Many people perceive it correctly as exactly the way it's intended, as a firm statement that you had better watch out, we're on the way. That's why the United States is now regarded as the greatest threat to peace in the world by probably the vast majority of the population of the world. George Bush has succeeded within a year in converting the United States into a country that is greatly feared, disliked, and even hated.

DAVID BARSAMIAN: At the World Social Forum in Porto Alegre in late January, you described Bush and the people around him as "radical nationalists" engaging in "imperial violence." Is this regime in Washington substantively different from previous ones?

NOAM CHOMSKY: It is useful to have some historical perspective. So let's go to the opposite end of the political spectrum, the Kennedy liberals, about as far as you can get. In 1963, they announced a doctrine which is not very different from Bush's national security strategy report. This was in 1963. Dean Acheson, a respected elder statesman, a senior adviser to the Kennedy administration, delivered a lecture to the American Society for International Law in which he instructed them that no legal challenge arises in the case of a U.S. response to a challenge to its position, prestige, or authority. The wording was pretty much like that. What was he referring to? He was referring to the U.S. terrorist war and economic warfare against Cuba. And the timing is quite significant. This was shortly after the missile crisis, which drove the world to the edge of nuclear war. And that was largely a result of a major campaign of international terrorism aimed at what's now called regime change, a major factor that led to the missiles being sent. Right afterwards, Kennedy stepped up the international terrorist campaign, and Acheson informed the Society for International Law that we had the right of preventive war against a mere challenge to our position and prestige, not even a threat to our existence. His wording, in fact, was even more extreme than the Bush doctrine last September.

On the other hand, to put it in perspective, that was a proclamation by Dean Acheson. It wasn't an official statement of policy. And it's obviously not the first or last declaration of this kind. This one last September is unusual in its brazenness and in the fact that it is a formal statement of policy, not just a statement by a high official.

DAVID BARSAMIAN: A slogan we have all heard at peace rallies is "No blood for oil." The whole issue of oil is often referred to as the driving force behind the U.S. attack and occupation of Iraq. How central is oil to U.S. strategy?

NOAM CHOMSKY: It's undoubtedly central. I don't think any sane person doubts that. The Gulf region is the main energy-producing region of the world. It has been since the Second World War. It's expected to be at least for another generation. It's a huge source of strategic power, of material wealth. And Iraq is absolutely central to it. It has the second largest oil reserves. It's very easily accessible, cheap. To control Iraq is to be in a very strong position to determine the price and production levels, not too high, not too low, to probably undermine OPEC, and to swing your weight around throughout the world. That's been true since the Second World War. It has nothing in particular to do with access to the oil; the U.S. doesn't really intend to access it. But it does have to do with control. So that's in the background. If Iraq was somewhere in Central Africa, it wouldn't be chosen for this test case. So that's certainly there in the background, just as it's there in less crucial regions, like Central Asia. However, it doesn't account for the specific timing of the operation, because that's a constant concern.

DAVID BARSAMIAN: A 1945 State Department document on Middle East oil described it as "a stupendous source of strategic power, and one of the greatest material prizes in world history." The U.S. imports 15 percent of its oil from Venezuela. It also imports oil from Colombia and Nigeria. All three of those states are perhaps, from Washington's perspective, somewhat problematic right now, with Hugo Chavez in Venezuela and serious internal conflicts, literally civil war, in Colombia, and uprisings in Nigeria threatening oil supplies there. What do you think about all of those factors?

NOAM CHOMSKY: That's very pertinent, and those are the regions where the U.S. actually intends to have access. The Middle East it wants to control. But, at least according to intelligence projections, the U.S. intends to rely on what they regard as more stable Atlantic Basin resources—Atlantic Basin means West Africa and the Western Hemisphere—which are more totally under U.S. control than the Middle East, which is a difficult region. So the projections are: control the Middle East, but maintain access to the Atlantic Basin, including the countries you mentioned. It does, therefore, follow that lack of conformity, disruption of one kind or another, in those areas is a significant threat, and there is very likely to be another episode like Iraq, if this one works the way the civilian planners at the Pentagon hope. If it's an easy victory, no fighting, establish a new regime which you will call democratic, and not too much catastrophe, if it works like that, they are going to be emboldened on to the next step.

And the next step, you can think of several possibilities. One of them, indeed, is the Andean region. The U.S. has military bases all around it now. There are military forces right in there. Colombia and Venezuela are both, especially Venezuela, substantial oil producers, and there is more elsewhere, like Ecuador, and even Brazil. Yes, that's a possibility, that the next step in the campaign of preventive wars, once the so-called norm is established and accepted, would be to go on there. Another possibility is Iran.

DAVID BARSAMIAN: Indeed, Iran. The U.S. was advised by none other than that, as Bush called him, "man of peace," Sharon, to go after Iran "the day after" they finish with Iraq. What about Iran? A designated axis-of-evil state and also a country that has a lot of oil.

NOAM CHOMSKY: As far as Israel is concerned, Iraq has never been much of an issue. They consider it a kind of pushover. But Iran is a different story. Iran is a much more serious military and economic force. And for years Israel has been pressing the United States to take on Iran. Iran is too big for Israel to attack, so they want the big boys to do it.

And it's quite likely that the war may already be under way. A year ago, over 10 percent of the Israeli air force was reported to be permanently based in eastern Turkey, that is, in these huge U.S. military bases in eastern Turkey. And they are reported to be flying reconnaissance over the Iranian border. In addition, there are credible reports that there are efforts, that the U.S. and Turkey and Israel are attempting to stir up Azeri nationalist forces in northern Iran to move towards a kind of a linkage of parts of Iran with Azerbaijan. There is a kind of an axis of U.S.–Turkish–Israeli power in the region opposed to Iran that may ultimately, perhaps, lead to the split-up of Iran and maybe military attack. Although there will be a military attack only if it's taken for granted that Iran would be basically defenseless. They're not going to invade anyone who can fight back.

DAVID BARSAMIAN: With U.S. military forces in Afghanistan and in Iraq, as well as bases in Turkey and Central Asia, Iran is literally surrounded now. Might not that objective reality on the ground push forces inside Iran to develop nuclear weapons, if they don't already have them, in self-defense?

NOAM CHOMSKY: Very likely. The little evidence we have—serious evidence—indicates that the 1981 Israeli bombing of the Osirak reactor probably stimulated and may have initiated the Iraqi nuclear weapons development program. They were engaged in building a nuclear plant, but what it was nobody knew. It was investigated on the ground after the bombing by a well-known nuclear physicist from Harvard—I believe he was head of the Harvard physics department at the time. He published his analysis in the leading scientific journal, *Nature*. According to him, it was a power plant. He's an expert on this topic. Other Iraqi sources, exiled, have indicated—we can't prove it—that nothing much was going on. They may have been toying with the idea of nuclear weapons, but that the bombing of it did stimulate the nuclear weapons program. You can't prove this, but that's what the evidence looks like. And it's very plausible. That doesn't have to be true. What you described is highly likely. If you come out and say, "Look, we're going to attack you," and countries know that they have no means of conventional defense, you're virtually ordering them to develop weapons of mass destruction and networks of terror. It's transparent. That's exactly why the CIA and everyone else predicted it.

DAVID BARSAMIAN: What does the Iraq war and occupation mean for the Palestinians?

NOAM CHOMSKY: Disaster.

DAVID BARSAMIAN: No roadmaps to peace?

NOAM CHOMSKY: It's interesting to read it. One of the rules of journalism—I don't know exactly how it got established, but it's held with absolute consistency—is that when you mention George Bush's name in an article, the headline has to speak of his vision and the article has to talk about his dreams. Maybe there will be a photograph of him right next to it peering into the distance. And one of George Bush's dreams and visions is to have a Palestinian state somewhere, sometime, in some unspecified place, maybe in the desert. And we are supposed to worship and praise that as a magnificent vision. It has become a convention of journalists. There was a lead story in the *Wall Street Journal* on March 21 which I think had the words "vision" and "dream" about ten times.

The vision and the dream is that maybe the United States will stop undermining totally the long-term efforts of the rest of the world, virtually without exception, to create some kind of a viable political settlement. Up until now, the United States has been blocking it, for the last twenty-five to thirty years. The Bush administration went even further in blocking it, sometimes in pretty extreme ways, so extreme that they weren't even reported.

For example, last December at the U.N., for the first time, the Bush administration reversed U.S. policy on Jerusalem. Up until now, the United States had, at least in principle, gone along with the 1968 Security Council resolution ordering Israel to revoke its annexation and occupation and settlement policies in East Jerusalem. And for the first time, last December, the Bush administration reversed that. That's one of many cases intended to undermine the possibility of any meaningful political settlement. To disguise this, it's called a vision, and the effort to pursue it is called a U.S. initiative, although in fact what it really is, as anyone who pays the slightest attention to the history knows, is a U.S. effort to catch up to long-standing European and Arab efforts and to try to cut them down so they don't mean very much. The great praise for Sharon in the United States, who is now considered a great statesman—he is, after all, one of the leading terrorist commanders in the world for the last fifty years—that's an interesting phenomenon, and it reveals another substantial achievement of propaganda, the whole story, and a dangerous one.

In mid-March, Bush made what was called his first significant pronouncement on the Middle East, on the Arab–Israeli problem. He gave a speech. Big headlines. First significant statement in years. If you read it, it was boilerplate, except for one sentence. That one sentence, if you take a look at it closely, gives his roadmap: as the peace process advances, Israel should terminate new settlement programs. What does that mean? That means until the peace process reaches a point that Bush endorses, which could be indefinitely far in the future, until then Israel should continue to build settlements. That's a change in policy. Up until now, officially at least, the U.S. has been opposed to expansion of the illegal settlement programs that make a political settlement impossible. But now Bush is saying the opposite: Go on and settle. We'll keep paying for it, until we decide that somehow the peace process has reached an adequate point. So, yes, it was a significant change towards more aggression, undermining of international law, and undermining of the possibilities of peace. That's not the way it was portrayed. But take a look at the wording.

DAVID BARSAMIAN: You've described the level of public protest and resistance to the Iraq war as "unprecedented"; never before has there been so much opposition before a war began. Where is that resistance going?

NOAM CHOMSKY: I don't know any way to predict human affairs. It will go the way people decide it will go. There are many possibilities. It should intensify. The tasks are now much greater and more serious than they were before. On the other hand, it's harder. It's just psychologically easier to organize to oppose a military attack than it is to oppose a long-standing program of imperial ambition, of which this attack is one phase, and of which others are going to come next. That takes more thought, more dedication, more long-term engagement. It's the difference between deciding, okay, I'm in this for the long haul and saying, OK, I'm going out to a demonstration tomorrow and then back home. Those are choices, all of them. The same in the civil rights movement, the women's movement, anything.

DAVID BARSAMIAN: Talk about threats to and intimidation of dissidents here inside the United States, including roundups of immigrants, and citizens, for that matter.

NOAM CHOMSKY: Vulnerable people like immigrants, definitely have to be concerned. The current government has claimed rights which go beyond any precedents. There are some in wartime, but those are pretty ugly ones, like the 1942 roundup of Japanese, or, say, Wilson during the First World

War, which was pretty awful. But they're now claiming rights that are quite without precedent, including even the right to arrest citizens, hold them in detention without access to family or lawyers, and do so indefinitely, without charges. Immigrants and other vulnerable people should certainly be cautious. On the other hand, for people like us, citizens with any privileges, though there are threats, as compared with what people face in most of the world, they are so slight that it's hard to get very upset about them. I've just been back from Turkey a couple of times and Colombia, and compared with the threats that people face there, we're living in heaven. And they don't worry about it. They do, obviously, but they don't let it stop them.

DAVID BARSAMIAN: Do you see Europe and East Asia emerging as counterforces to U.S. power at some point?

NOAM CHOMSKY: They're emerging all right. There is no doubt that Europe and Asia are economic forces roughly on a par with North America, and have their own interests. Their interests are not simply to follow U.S. orders. They're tightly linked. So, for example, the corporate sector in Europe, the U.S., and most of Asia are linked in all kinds of ways and have common interests. On the other hand, there are separate interests, and these are problems that go way back, especially with Europe.

The U.S. has always had an ambivalent attitude towards Europe. It wanted Europe to be unified, as a more efficient market for U.S. corporations, great advantages of scale. On the other hand, it was always concerned about the threat that Europe might move off in another direction. A lot of the issues about the accession of the East European countries to the European Union have a lot to do with that. The U.S. is strongly in favor of it, because it's hoping that these countries will be more susceptible to U.S. influence and will be able to undermine the core of Europe, which is France and Germany, the big industrial countries, which might move in a somewhat more independent direction.

Also in the background is a long-standing U.S. hatred of the European social market system, which provides decent wages and working conditions and benefits. It's very different from the U.S. system. And they don't want that model to exist, because it's a dangerous one. People get funny ideas. And it's very explicitly stated that with the accession of Eastern European countries, with low wages and repression of labor and so on, it may help undermine the social and worker standards in Western Europe, and that would be a big benefit for the U.S.

DAVID BARSAMIAN: With the U.S. economy deteriorating and with more layoffs, how is the Bush administration going to maintain what some are calling a garrison state with permanent war and occupation of numerous countries? How are they going to pull it off?

NOAM CHOMSKY: They have to pull it off for about another six years. By that time they hope they will have institutionalized highly reactionary programs within the United States. They will have left the economy in a very serious state, with huge deficits, pretty much the way they did in the 1980s. And then it will be somebody else's problem to patch it together. Meanwhile, they will have, they hope, undermined social programs, diminished democracy, which of course they hate, by transferring decisions out of the public arena into private hands. And they will have done it in a way that will be very hard to disentangle. So they will have left a legacy internally that will be painful and hard. But only for the majority of the population. The people they're concerned about are going to be making out like bandits. Very much like the Reagan years. It's the same people, after all.

And internationally, they hope that they will have institutionalized the doctrines of imperial domination through force and preventive war as a choice. The U.S. now in military spending probably exceeds the rest of the world combined, and it's much more advanced and moving out into extremely dangerous directions, like space. They assume, I suppose, that no matter what happens to the American economy, that will give such overwhelming force that people will just have to do what they say.

DAVID BARSAMIAN: What do you say to the peace activists who labored for so long trying to prevent the invasion of Iraq and who are now feeling a sense of anger and sadness?

NOAM CHOMSKY: That they should be realistic. Abolitionism. How long did the struggle go on before they made any progress? If you give up every time you don't achieve the immediate gain you want, you're just guaranteeing that the worst is going to happen. These are long, hard struggles. And, in fact, what happened in the last couple of months should be seen quite positively. The basis was created for expansion and development of a peace and justice movement that will move on to much harder tasks. And that's the way these things go. It isn't easy.

3

The Grid of History, Cowboys and Indians

ROXANNE DUNBAR-ORTIZ

We were like Custer. We were surrounded.

—SERGEANT JAMES J. RILEY explaining why he ordered surrender in an engagement in Nasiriyah, Iraq, on March 23, 2003.[1]

At the onset of the U.S. military invasion of Iraq, Senator Robert Byrd emotionally queried: "What is happening to this country? When did we become a nation which ignores and berates our friends? When did we decide to risk undermining international order by adopting a radical and doctrinaire approach to using our awesome military might? How can we abandon diplomacy when the turmoil in the world cries out for diplomacy?"

As a historian, I would have to respond to Senator Byrd that 1776 or thereabouts was when. Many admirable U.S. anti-imperialists have been making the same point as Senator Byrd. An erasure of history is at the heart of some of the most anti-imperialist critiques of the Bush administration's foreign policy. Continuity is hidden, and a small departure is exaggerated. From Gore Vidal to Manning Marable to Michael Moore, "lost democracy" is a refrain. Edward Said writes: "The doctrine of military preemption was never voted on by the American people or their representatives . . . It seems so monumentally criminal that important words like democracy and freedom have been hijacked, used as a mask for pillage, taking over territory and settling scores." Said ends his essay by, correctly, stating: "Bush looks like a cowboy."[2]

That observation is also common to critics of the war around the world. Although it is meant to be understood as a *bad* thing, in fact, the cowboy is not a negative metaphor for many U.S. citizens, particularly those who are descendants of the old settler class, as are the majority of the ruling class and officers of the military. How many generations of children now have grown up gleefully playing cowboys and Indians?

Perhaps the fact that I grew up as a child of a cowboy father and Indian mother narrows my view of this metaphor, making it loom too large and out of perspective. Then again, maybe that experience brings with it some insider knowledge.

THE RISE OF WHITE SUPREMACY AND IMPERIALISM/CAPITALISM

To allow no dissent from the truth was exactly the reason they had come to America.

Are your garments spotless?
Are they white as snow?
Are they washed in the blood of the lamb?[3]

As this traditional evangelical Christian hymn suggests, whiteness as an ideology is far more complex than mere skin color, although skin color has been and continues to be a key component of racism within the United States. The origins of white supremacy as it is now experienced and institutionalized—and denied—in the United States (and, due to colonialism and imperialism, throughout the world) can be traced to the prior colonizing ventures of Christian Crusades into Muslim-controlled territories, and to the Calvinist Protestant colonization of Ireland. These were the models for the colonization of the western hemisphere, and they are the two strands that merge in the genetic makeup of U.S. society.

The Christian Crusades against Islam/Africa gave birth to the law of *limpieza de sangre*, cleanliness of blood, which the Spanish Inquisition was mandated to investigate and determine. The Christian Crusades, particularly the Castilian conquest of the Iberian Peninsula and expulsion of Jews and Muslims, created the seed ideology and institutions for modern colonialism with its necessary tools—racist ideology and justification for genocide. The law of *limpieza de sangre* was perhaps the most important cargo on the 1492 voyage of Christopher Columbus, sailing under the flag of Spain.

Great Britain emerged as an overseas colonial power a century later than Spain and absorbed aspects of the Spanish caste system into its colonialist rationalizations, particularly regarding African slavery, within the context of chosen people/New Jerusalem Calvinism and Puritanism.

In the pre-formation of the United States, Puritanism and Calvinist Protestantism uniquely refined white supremacy as a political/religious ideology (a covenant with God) requiring the shedding of white blood for purification. The Ulster-Scots Calvinists were the settlers/colonizers of Northern Ireland and constituted a majority of settlers in the western lands over the Appalachian/Allegheny spine of English North America. Their origin story became the origin story of the United States. It tells of pilgrim/settlers doing God's will and forging into the promised land, being surrounded by savages, and killing the heathen (first the Irish in Ulster, then the Native Americans in North America). Thereby, the sacrifice and blood shed is perceived as proof of the sanctity and purity of the nation itself. All the descendants of those who made such sacrifices are the true inheritors of the land.

THE CRUSADES AND PURITY OF BLOOD

In the eighth century, Muslims came to power in all but the northern fringe of the Iberian Peninsula and ruled for centuries. However, by the end of the fifteenth century, the last Muslim state held only a foothold in Granada, an enclave on the southeastern coast surrounded by the expansionist Christian monarchies of Castile and Aragon. During those intervening seven hundred years, various Christian kingdoms based in the north of the peninsula attacked Moorish territory, seizing their lands and properties. The Christian crusaders named this process *La Reconquista*, the reconquest. This military/religious project created the institutions and practices later established in Spanish America, especially the *encomienda* (conquered land granted to the conquistador along with the people on it, with the conquistador earning the noble title of hidalgo). As Henry Kamen tells us:

> The Reconquest meant the slow and systematic extension of Christian power over all those lands that had been Muslim since the eighth century, and so involved the clash of Christian and Muslim armies and societies. What the Reconquest destroyed, however, was the racial and religious coexistence, which despite incessant armed conflict had distinguished the society of mediaeval Spain. It was claimed by a contemporary that when the Christians went to war against the Moors, it was "neither because of the law (of Mahommed) nor because of the sect that they hold to," but because of the lands they occupied and for this reason alone.[4]

Before Christian aggression and eventual expulsion of the Moors from the Iberian Peninsula, Christians, Jews, and Muslims had enjoyed a mutual tolerance so the question of racial or religious conflict had not existed.

The Vatican created the original institution of the Inquisition in 1179 for rooting out Christian heretics, the original mandate being free of racialization. However, the fifteenth century in Spain saw increasing Inquisition investigations of *conversos*, that is, Christian-converted Jews, and of *moriscos*, Christian-converted Muslims. Jews and Muslims who refused to convert were finally deported en masse from the Iberian Peninsula at the end of the fifteenth century. (It is said that Columbus watched the people being loaded on to ships for deportation as he set sail in 1492.)

Before this time the concept of biological race based on "blood" is not known to have existed as law or taboo in Christian Europe or anywhere else in the world.[5] As scapegoating and suspicion of *conversos* and *moriscos* intensified in Christian Spain, the doctrine of *limpieza de sangre* was popularized and had the effect of granting psychological, and increasingly legal, privileges to "Old Christians," thereby obscuring the class differences between the poor and the rich, that is, between the landed aristocracy and the land-poor peasants and shepherds. In Cervantes' *Don Quixote* the impoverished Sancho Panza says, "I am an Old Christian, and to become an earl that is sufficient," to which Don Quixote replies, "And more than sufficient." And Cervantes' contemporary, Lope de Vega, wrote in his *Peribá*ñez: "soy un hombre, / aunque de villana casta, / limpio de sangre y jam / de hebrea o mora manchada" (I am a man, although of lowly status, yet clean of blood and with no mixture of Jewish or Moorish blood.)

What we witness in late-fifteenth- and early-sixteenth-century Spain is the first instance of class leveling based on imagined biological racial differences, indeed the origin of white supremacy, the necessary ideology of colonial projects in America and Africa. We see here the beginnings of the "thousand-year Reich" of settler capitalism/colonialism, and its characteristic tug-of-war over the hearts and minds of the majority of the settlers—the yeomanry, and later the "white" working classes. Historian David Stannard, in his *American Holocaust*, adds to Elie Wiesel's famous observation that the road to Auschwitz was paved in the earliest days of Christendom, the *caveat* that on the way to Auschwitz the road led straight through the heart of America.[6] The ideology of white supremacy was paramount in neutralizing the class antagonisms of the landless against the landed, and in the distribution of the confiscated lands and properties of Moors, Jews, and of Irish, Native Americans and Africans. Kamen describes the process in fifteenth- and sixteenth-century Spain:

> a situation in which the highest and lowest classes could maintain social mobility without great fear of social distinction...as with the genuine aristocracy, the concepts of honour, pride and *hidalgu 'EDa* become the very foundations of action. . . In so far as this concept of honour was identified with the virtues of the Old Christian nobility, deference to honour became deference to the nobility . . . the Castilian nobility continued to regard their functions as essentially the same that they had always been. Their task was to fight and not to labour. *Hidalgu 'EDa* would not permit a nobleman, even the lowest rank of nobleman, to labour or to trade.[7]

The "Old Christian" Spanish, whatever their economic situation, were allowed to identify with the worldview of the nobility. As one Spanish historian puts it, "The common people looked upwards, wishing and hoping to climb, and let themselves be seduced by chivalric ideals: honour, dignity, glory, and the noble life."[8]

We can also locate the origin of genocide and its linkage to colonialism in the late fifteenth century in Spain. Two punishments were devised to root out uncertain Christians deemed to have unclean blood: the extermination of many burned at the stake and the social isolation and persecution of the rest.

IRELAND AND THE ENGLISH INQUISITION

During the early seventeenth century the English conquered Northern Ireland, and declared a half-million acres of land open to settlement; the settlers who contracted with the devil of early colonialism came mostly from western Scotland. England had previously conquered Wales and southern and eastern Ireland, but had never previously attempted on such a scale to remove the indigenous population and "plant" settlers. The English policy of exterminating Indians in North America was foreshadowed by this English colonization of Northern Ireland. The ancient Irish social system was systematically attacked, traditional songs and music forbidden, whole clans exterminated, and the remainder brutalized. A "wild Irish" reservation was even attempted.[9] The planted settlers were Calvinist Protestants, assured by their divines that they had been chosen by God for salvation (and title to the lands of Ulster). The native (and Papist) Irish were definitely not destined for salvation, but rather the reverse, both in the present and hereafter.

The "plantation" of Ulster followed centuries of intermittent warfare in Ireland, and was as much the culmination of a process as a departure. In the sixteenth century, the official in charge of the Irish province of Munster, Sir Humphrey Gilbert, ordered that:

> The heddes of all those (of what sort soever thei were) which were killed in the daie, should be cutte off from their bodies and brought to the place where he incamped at night, and should there bee laied on the ground by eche side of the waie ledying into his owne tente so that none could come into his tente for any cause but commonly he muste passe through a lane of heddes which he used ad terrorem...[It brought] greate terrour to the people when thei sawe the heddes of their dedde fathers, brothers, children, kindsfolke, and freinds.[10]

Bounties were paid for the Irish heads brought in and later only the scalp or ears were required. A century later, in North America, Indian heads and scalps were brought in for bounty in the same manner. Native Americans picked up the practice from the colonizers. The first English colonial settlement in North America had been planted in Newfoundland in the summer of 1583, by Sir Humphrey Gilbert.

During the mid-nineteenth century, influenced by Social Darwinism, some English scientists peddled the theory that the Irish (and of course all people of color) had descended from apes, while the English were descendants of man who had been created by God in His image. Thus the English were "angels" and the Irish (and other colonized peoples) were a lower species, what today U.S. white supremacists call "mud people," products of the process of evolution.[11] It is the seventeenth-century Ulster Calvinist ideology in late-nineteenth-century modern guise.

WHITE SUPREMACY, THE U.S. ORIGIN MYTH, AND U.S. IMPERIALISM

Two paragraphs, rarely cited, from the Declaration of Independence raise thorny questions about Anglo-American imperialist roots in forming the breakaway United States of America. This was not simply the founding of a republic for propertied, mostly slave-owning, white males, but more importantly a settler-colonialist and imperialist-aggressor state.

> He [King George] has endeavored to prevent the population of these States; for that purpose, obstructing the laws for naturalization of foreigners, refusing to pass others to encourage their migration hither, and raising the conditions of new appropriations of lands. [The treaty ending the French and Indian War made British settlement over the Allegheny/Appalachian line into Indian country illegal and ordered the return of those tens of thousand settlers who had already squatted there, demanding land rights.] He has excited domestic insurrections amongst us and has endeavored to bring on the

> inhabitants of our frontiers, the merciless Indian savages, whose known rule of warfare is an undistinguished destruction of all ages, sexes, and conditions.

Not only did founding father Thomas Jefferson pen those words, he was also the real architect of the genocide and confiscation of the land of settled indigenous peoples later termed the Jacksonian policy of Indian removal.

Reconciling empire and liberty was a historic obsession of U.S. political thinkers and historians, and in the twenty-first century it is openly being debated once again. Thomas Jefferson had hailed the United States as an "empire for liberty." Andrew Jackson coined the phrase "extending the area of freedom" to describe the process in which slavery had been introduced into Texas in violation of governing Mexican laws, to be quickly followed by a slaveholder's rebellion and U.S. annexation. The term *freedom* became a euphemism for the continental and worldwide expansion of the world's leading slave power. The contradictions, particularly since the initial rationalization for U.S. independence was anti-empire, are multiple.

It is easy to date U.S. imperialism to Andrew Jackson, but he only carried out the original plan, initially as an army general who led three genocidal wars against the Muskogee in Georgia/Florida, then as the most popular president ever, and the organizer of the expulsion of all native peoples east of the Mississippi to the Oklahoma Territory.

Although white supremacy was the working rationalization and ideology behind theft of Native American lands, and especially the justification for African slavery, the independence bid by what became the United States of America is more problematic, in that democracy/equality and supremacy/dominance/empire do not make an easy fit. During the 1820s, in the era of Jacksonian Democracy, the unique U.S. origin myth was created, with James Fenimore Cooper as the initial scribe. Cooper's reinvention of America in *The Last of the Mohicans* has become the official U.S. story. Herman Melville called Cooper "our national novelist," and he was the great hero of Walt Whitman who sang the song of manhood and the American superrace through empire. As a supporter of the U.S. war against Mexico, 1846–1848, Whitman proposed the stationing of sixty thousand U.S. troops in Mexico to establish a regime change there, "whose efficiency and permanency shall be guaranteed by the United States. This will bring out enterprise, open the way for manufacturers and commerce, into which the immense dead capital of the country will find its way."[12]

Whitman's sentiment followed the already established U.S. origin myth that had the frontier settlers replacing the native peoples, similar to the parallel Afrikaner origin myth in South Africa.

To the extent that African Americans, Native Americans, Chicanos, Puerto Ricans, and non-European immigrants are allowed (and are willing) to embrace and embody U.S. patriotism, they may be accepted as *conversos*, as the Spanish Inquisition termed those who professed Christianity despite their "unclean" blood. Yet in the end, only the Old Settlers are true Americans.

This white supremacist ideology formed the core of U.S. foreign policy as well, from its origins to the present. As Samir Amin pointed out: "During this entire phase [the cold war] the East–West conflict was presented as a struggle between socialism and capitalism, although it was never anything other than the conflict between the periphery and the center, manifested in its most radical form."[13]

WHY DO WE DATE U.S. IMPERIALISM ONLY TO 1898, AND AS AN ABERRATION?

American supremacy and populist imperialism are inseparable from the content of the U.S. origin story and the definition of patriotism in the United States today. And it began at the beginning, even before the founding of the United States, not as an accident or aberration in the progression of democracy. The founding of the United States marked a split in the British Empire, not an anticolonial liberation movement.

The very term *frontier*, used to define the border between independent Native American nations and the United States, implies a foreign country on the other side of a demarcation line—a country to be invaded, its inhabitants controlled and then expelled, while settlers move in protected by the army. Everything accounted for in the first hundred years or more as "movement of the frontier" was plain and simple imperialism, fitting all the definitions thereof.

During this new phase of U.S. imperialism following 9/11, accelerating with the invasion, occupation, and administration of Iraq, commentators and historians—left and right—but mostly liberal Democrats, observe that the United States is not very good at imperialism, with vague references to the Spanish-American War. Actually, the United States has not become the most powerful military machine and the most dominant power on earth and in history by accident or by staying home and minding the cows and banks like the Swiss, who are capitalist and rich, but not imperialists.

"Well, so what?" many of my antiwar and social-justice friends ask me, asserting that the truth would alienate "ordinary people," whoever they are. Who would know since it has never been tried? Besides, I have my doubts that most of my leftist friends are themselves prepared to accept that the very origin of the United States is fundamentally imperialist, rather than imperialism being a divergence from a well-intentioned path. The public acceptance of media propaganda justifying U.S. government aggression falls into the pattern of a belief system based on the origin story that is uninterrupted and uninterrogated by us, the left.

Of course, there are many leftist and social democratic thinkers and scholars who challenge the 1898 age-of-imperialism myth. Most notably, *Monthly Review* has never strayed from understanding the long history of U.S. imperialism, particularly in Latin America. Also, William Appleman Williams and a whole generation of radical U.S. historians acknowledge "empire as a way of life," the title of Williams' 1980 book of essays that includes an exhaustive list of overseas interventions dating back to day one, giving substance to the U.S. Marine Corps hymn's invocation of "the shores of Tripoli."[14] And with the Iraq intervention, many antiwar critics have compiled such lists.

The expansion of the United States from sea to shining sea is coming under reexamination, even from bourgeois historians, with the sudden unabashed assertion of U.S. imperialism. Warren Zimmermann, in his recent book on the frankly imperial aims of the Teddy Roosevelt administration, introduces his material with words rarely found in mainstream literature:

> Americans like to pretend that they have no imperial past. Yet they have shown expansionist tendencies since colonial days . . . Overland expansion, often at the expense of Mexicans and Indians, was a marked feature of American history right through the period of the Civil War, by which time the United States had reached its continental proportions.
>
> The War for American Independence, which created most of the founding myths of the Republic, was itself a war for expansion . . . Thomas Jefferson nursed even grander plans for empire.[15]

Warren Zimmermann himself knows something of the practical side of imperialism. He was the last U.S. ambassador to pre–civil war Yugoslavia. Surely it is past time for leftists to abandon the Whitmanesque celebratory myths of a democratic American manifest destiny.

CONCLUSION

As a graduate student in Latin American history at UCLA in the mid-1960s, I first learned about imperialism, and it was my good fortune to have access to Marxist analysis. However, it was not until the early 1970s, when I became involved as an expert witness in Native American court cases regarding U.S.–Indian treaties, that I came to grasp the true nature and development of U.S. imperialism. At that same time, a now deceased mentor, Canadian Native leader and Marxist historian, Howard Adams, gave me a book that had a great influence on me.[16] That book was Pierre Jalée's *Imperialism in the Seventies,* which contained a brilliant introduction by Harry Magdoff. Harry's cautionary words three decades ago resonate even more loudly today:

> The major obstacle to such enlightenment is the pervasiveness of the ideological rationalization for imperialism. The extent of this pervasiveness is not easy to perceive because such rationalization is deep-seated. Its roots are intertwined with the accepted, conventional modes of thought and the consciousness of a people. Thus, they are located in the false patriotism and racism that sink deeply and imperceptibly into the individual's sub-conscious; in the traditions, values, and even aesthetics of the cultural environment—an environment evolved over centuries during which self-designated "superior" cultures assumed the right to penetrate and dominate "inferior" cultures. These roots are also buried in the sophisticated theorems of both liberal and conservative economics, sociology, political science, anthropology, and history. For these reasons, citizens of an imperialist country who wish to understand imperialism must first emancipate themselves from the seemingly endless web of threads that bind them emotionally and intellectually to the imperialist condition.[17]

This, I believe, is the most important task for the antiwar and social-justice movements in the United States today—to assume the responsibility of being citizens of an empire that must be dismantled.

4

U.S. Weakness and the Struggle for Hegemony

IMMANUEL WALLERSTEIN

Imperialism is an integral part of the capitalist world economy. It is not a special phenomenon. It has always been there. It always will be there as long as we have a capitalist world economy. However, today we are experiencing a particularly aggressive and egregious form of imperialism, which is now even ready to claim that it is being imperialist.

Let us reflect upon that anomaly. Why are we now living through a particularly aggressive and egregious form of imperialism, which for the first time in over a hundred years has been ready to use the words "imperial," and "imperialism"? The answer most people give in one word is U.S. *strength*. And the answer I will give in one word is U.S. *weakness*.

We have to start in 1945 when the United States became truly hegemonic. What does hegemony in this context mean? At that time, the U.S. nation-state was so much the strongest; it had an economic capability so far ahead of anybody else in the world that it could undersell everyone in their own home markets. The United States had a military strength that was unparalleled. As a consequence, it had an ability to create formidable alliances, NATO, the U.S.-Japan Defense Pact, and so on. At the same time, the United States, as the hegemonic power, became culturally the center of the world. New York became the center of high culture, and American popular culture went on its march throughout the world.

The first time I was in the Soviet Union, in the Brezhnev era, my host took me to a nightclub in Leningrad. The one thing that startled me in the Soviet Union, the whole time I was there, was that in this nightclub one heard American popular music sung in English. And, of course, ideologically, I think we underestimate the degree to which the theme of the "free world" has had legitimacy among wide segments of the world population.

So the United States was really on top of the world for about twenty-five years, and it got its way in whatever it wanted to do.

It is true that there was the Soviet Union, which posed a military difficulty for the United States. Nonetheless, the United States handled that very simply by an agreement. It is called Yalta, which encompasses more than just what happened at Yalta itself. I think the left has underestimated historically the reality and the importance of the Yalta arrangements, which, in effect, made the cold war a choreographed arrangement in which nothing ever really happened for forty years. That was the important thing about the cold war. It divided up the world into a Soviet zone that was about a third of the world and a U.S. zone that was two-thirds. It kept the zones economically separate and allowed them to shout at each other loudly in order to keep their own side in order, but never to make any truly substantial changes in the arrangement.

This lasted only about twenty-five years. The United States ran into difficulty somewhere between 1967 and 1973 because of three things. One, it lost its economic edge. Western Europe and Japan became sufficiently strong to defend their own markets. They even began to invade U.S. markets. They were then about as economically powerful and as competitive as the United States, and that, of course, had political implications.

Second, there was the world revolution of 1968. In 1968, there were two themes that were repeated throughout the world in one version or another. One, we do not like U.S. hegemony and dominance of the world, and we don't like Soviet collusion with it. That was a theme everywhere. That was not only the Chinese stance on the two superpowers but that of most of the rest of the world as well.

The second theme of 1968 was that the Old Left, which had come to power everywhere—Communist parties, social-democratic parties, and national liberation movements—had not changed the world and something had to be done about it. We were not sure we trusted them anymore. That undermined the ideological basis of the Yalta agreement, and that was very important.

The third thing that happened between 1968 and 1973 is that there were people who did not agree with Yalta. They were located in the third world, and there were at least four significant defeats of imperialism that occurred in the third world. The first was China, where the Communist Party defied Stalin and marched on Kuomintang-controlled Shanghai in 1948, thus getting China out from under U.S. influence on the mainland. That was a central defeat in the U.S. attempt to control the periphery. Then there was Algeria and all its implications as a role model for other colonial territories.

There was Cuba, in the backyard of the United States. And finally there was Vietnam, which both France and then the United States were incapable of defeating. It was a military defeat for the United States that has structured world geopolitics ever since.

The threefold fact of the rise of economic rivals, the world revolution of 1968 and its impact on mentalities across the world, and Vietnam's defeat of the United States, all taken together, marks the beginning of the decline of the United States.

How could the rulers of the United States handle the loss of hegemony? That has been the problem ever since. There were two dominant modes of handling this loss of hegemony. One is that pursued from Nixon through Clinton, including Ronald Reagan and George Bush Sr. All these presidents of the United States handled it the same way, basically a variant of the velvet glove hiding the mailed fist.

In this approach, U.S. leaders sought to persuade Western Europe, Japan, and others that the United States can be cooperative, that the others could have an alliance of semi-equals, though with the United States exerting "leadership." That is the Trilateral Commission and the G7. And, of course, all that time they were using the unifying force of opposition to the Soviet Union.

The second mode of dealing with the loss of hegemony was the so-called Washington Consensus that coalesced in the 1980s. What is the Washington Consensus about? To understand it, we must first remember that the 1970s was the era when the United Nations proclaimed the decade of development. Developmentalism was the name of the game from the 1950s through the 1970s. Everybody proclaimed that countries could develop. The United States proclaimed it. The Soviet Union proclaimed it, and everybody in the third world proclaimed it—if only a state were organized properly. This was the basic ideology; development was to be achieved by some kind of control over what went on within sovereign national states.

Now the Washington Consensus was the abandonment and the denigration of developmentalism, which had visibly failed by the late 1980s, and, therefore, everyone was ready to abandon it. They substituted for developmentalism what they called globalization, which simply meant opening up all the frontiers, breaking down all the barriers for (a) the movement of goods; and more importantly, (b) capital; but not (c) labor. And the United States set out to impose this on the world.

An important element of the Washington Consensus was the ideological consensus-building process at Davos. Davos is not unimportant. Davos represents an attempt to create a meeting ground of the world's elites, including elites from the third world, and to constantly bring together and blend their political activity.

At the same time, the objectives of the United States during this period took three forms. One objective was to launch a counteroffensive, the counteroffensive of neoliberalism, which aimed to (1) reduce wages worldwide; (2) reduce costs to (and end ecological constraints on) corporations, permitting the total externalization and socialization of such costs; and (3) reduce taxation, which was subsidizing social welfare (that is to say subsidizing education, health care, and lifelong guarantees of income).

This counteroffensive was only partially successful. None of the three aims succeeded totally, but they all succeeded a little. However, cost curves were not brought down to anything like the 1945 level. The cost curves had gone way up and they are down now, but they are not down below the 1945 level, and they will go up again.

The second objective was to deal with the military threat. The real threat to U.S. military power is nuclear proliferation, because if every little country has nuclear weapons it becomes very tricky for the United States to engage in military action. That is what North Korea is demonstrating at this moment.

The third objective—very crucial and in the works since the 1970s—was to stop the European Union. The United States was for the European Union in the 1950s and 1960s when it was a means of getting France to agree to have Germany rearm. But once it became serious, it was viewed as an attempt to create a European state of one variety or another, and the United States was of course strongly opposed to it.

What happened? First, we had the collapse of the Soviet Union. That was a disaster for the United States; it removed the most important political weapon they had in relation to Western Europe and East Asia.

Second, there was Saddam. Saddam Hussein started the first Gulf War. He did it deliberately. He did it deliberately to challenge the United States. He could not have done that if the Soviet Union had still been an active power. They would have stopped him from doing it because it would have been too dangerous in terms of the Yalta agreement. And he got away with it. At the end of the war, all he lost was what he had gained. He was back at the starting point. That is what has stuck in their craw for ten years. That war was a draw. It was not a victory for the United States.

Third, we saw in the 1990s a momentary spurt of the U.S. economy, but not of the world economy as a whole. But we now have a weakening of the dollar, and the dollar has been a crucial lever of the United States, enabling it to have the kind of economy it has and the dominance it has over the rest of the world.

And finally, we had 9/11 which showed that the United States was vulnerable.

Enter the hawks. The hawks do not see themselves as the triumphant continuation of U.S. capitalism or U.S. power or anything else. They see themselves as a group of frustrated outsiders who for fifty years did not get their way even with Ronald Reagan, even with George Bush Sr., even with George Bush Jr. before 9/11. They are still worried that George Bush Jr. will chicken out on them. They think that the policy that went from Nixon to Clinton to the first year of George W. Bush, that of trying to handle this situation diplomatically and multilaterally—what I called above the velvet glove—was an utter failure. They think it just accelerated the decline of the United States, and they think that had to be changed radically by engaging in an egregious, overt, imperial action—war for the sake of war. They did not go to war on Iraq or Saddam Hussein because he was a dictator. They did not go to war on Iraq even for oil. I will not argue that point here, but they did not need the war on Iraq for oil. They needed it to show the United States could do it, and they needed that demonstration in order to intimidate two groups of people: (1) anybody in the third world who thinks that they should engage in nuclear proliferation and (2) Europe. This was an attack on Europe, and that is why Europe responded the way it did.

I wrote an article in 1980 in which I said, "It is geopolitically inevitable that over the next period, there will emerge a Paris/Berlin/Moscow alliance." I said this when the Soviet Union was still in existence, and I have repeated it ever since. Now, everybody talks about it. There is actually a website now (www.paris-berlin-moscou.info/) which reprints what people are writing in French, German, Russian, and English throughout Europe about the virtues of a Paris/Berlin/Moscow linkup.

We must not underestimate the second Security Council non-vote in March of this year. It is the first time since the United Nations was founded that the United States, on an issue that mattered to it, could not get a majority on the Security Council. Of course, it has had to veto various resolutions in the past but on no issue that was truly crucial to them. But in March 2003 it withdrew the resolution because it could not get more than four votes. It was a political humiliation, and it was universally regarded as such. The United States has lost legitimacy, and that is why you cannot call it hegemonic anymore. Whatever you want to call it, there is no legitimacy now, and that's crucial.

So, what should we look for in the next ten years? First, there is the question of how Europe will construct itself. It will be very difficult, but they will construct themselves and they will construct an army. Maybe not all of Europe, but the core. The United States is really worried about it, and that army will sooner or later link up with the Russian army.

Second, look at North East Asia. I think China, a reunited Korea, and Japan will begin to move together politically and economically. This will not be easy. The reunification of Korea will be a tremendously difficult thing to achieve. The reunification of China will also be a difficult thing to achieve, and those countries have all sorts of reasons for hating each other and tensions with deep historical roots, but the pressure is on them. If, realistically, they are going to survive as independent forces in the world, they will move in this direction.

Third, we should watch the World Social Forum. It is the most important social movement now on the face of the earth and the only one that has a chance of playing a really significant role. It has blossomed very fast. It has a wealth of internal contradictions that we should not underestimate and it will run through all sorts of difficult periods, and it may not make it. It may not survive as a movement that is a movement of movements, that has no hierarchical center, is tolerant of all the varieties within it, and yet stands for something. This is not an easy game, but it is where the best hope lies.

Finally, I would think you ought to look at the internal contradictions among capitalists. The basic political contradiction of capitalism throughout its history has been that all capitalists have a common political interest insofar as there is a worldwide class struggle going on. At the same time, all capitalists are rivals of all other capitalists. Now that is a fundamental contradiction of the system, and it is going to be very explosive.

I don't think we should underestimate the importance of the fact that in April 2003 Lawrence Eagleburger, the secretary of state under the first President Bush and still a close adviser to him, said in print that if the United States were now to invade Syria, he, Eagleburger, would be for impeaching George W. Bush. Now, that is not a very light thing for a person of that sort to say. So there is a message being sent, and who is the message coming from? I think it is coming from the father, for one thing. And beyond that, it is coming from an important segment of U.S. capital and of world capital. They are not all happy about the hawks. The hawks have not won the game. They have grabbed hold of the U.S. state machinery; 9/11 made that possible. And the hawks know it is now or never and they will continue to push, because if they don't push forward, they will fall back. But they have no guarantee of success, and some of their biggest enemies are other capitalists who do not like the line with Europe and Japan because they basically do believe in the unity of capital, who don't think that the way you handle these things is by smashing all opposition, but would prefer to co-opt it. They are extremely worried that this is Samson pulling down the house.

We have entered a chaotic world. This chaotic world situation will go on for the next twenty or thirty years. No one controls it, least of all the United States government. The United States government is adrift in a situation that it is trying to manage all over the place and that it will be incapable of managing. This is neither good nor bad, but we should not overestimate these people nor the strength on which they rely.

PART TWO

The Geopolitics and Political Economy of U.S. Imperialism

The imperialism practiced by the few rich capitalist countries has created a world sharply divided into rich and poor nations. One of the purposes of such international domination is for the rich nations to exert enough control over the poor nations to ensure that the latter's resources—oil, minerals, land, water—are available for exploitation by the corporations of the rich countries and to make certain that the capital of these corporations finds a welcome home anywhere it chooses to go. Control is exerted where necessary by military force, and this is always ready to be used should the poor nations try to become more than nominally independent. But under normal circumstances the everyday working of the market by and large maintains imperial power.

The imperialist nations are not of course a homogeneous group. The capitals in each of these states compete with those of every other leading capitalist state. This competition is at the heart of what Michael Klare calls "geopolitics." As history shows us, sometimes these inter- imperial rivalries become so intense that they generate wars. At other times, one imperial power becomes so dominant that it is able to become a hegemonic power. It uses its superior economic, political, and military force to impose a status quo of its own making on other imperial powers, dictating relations between the rich and poor nations.

Since the Second World War the hegemonic power has been the United States. Not only is its economy the largest and most dominant in the world but its military machine can only be described as without precedent. The United States has used its power to force entry of its capital into nearly every country in the world. It has, in addition, achieved the enviable state of possessing the world's primary currency—the U.S. dollar. This has allowed the United States to do what no other country can do: It can run persistent deficits in its balance of payments without the repercussions any other country would face. The power of the dollar is a critical element in the political economy of imperialism.

With the demise of the Soviet Union, the United States has found itself without a counterweight to its military power, though in the economic sphere it has powerful rivals. In these circumstances it has become increasingly willing to use its military power in the hope of strengthening its overall hegemony. But as the invasion and occupation of Iraq demonstrates, this creates new contradictions that will likely destabilize the world system and the United States itself.

5

The New Geopolitics

MICHAEL KLARE

The war in Iraq has reconfigured the global geopolitical landscape in many ways, some of which may not be apparent for years or even decades to come. It has certainly altered the United States' relationship with Europe and the Middle East. But its impact goes well beyond this. More than anything else, the war reveals that the new central pivot of intra-capitalist competition is the south-central area of Eurasia.

The term *geopolitics* seems at first to come from another era, from the late nineteenth century. By geopolitics or geopolitical competition, I mean the contention among great powers and aspiring great powers for control over territory, resources, and important geographical positions, such as ports and harbors, canals, river systems, oases, and other sources of wealth and influence. If you look back, you will find that this kind of contestation has been the driving force in world politics and especially world conflict in much of the past few centuries.

Geopolitics, as a mode of analysis, was very popular from the late nineteenth century into the early part of the twentieth century. If you studied then what academics now call international relations, you were studying geopolitics.

Geopolitics died out as a self-conscious mode of analysis in the Cold War period, partly due to echoes of the universally abhorred Hitlerite ideology of *lebensraum*, but also because there were a lot of parallels between classical geopolitical thinking (which came out of a conservative wing of academia) and Marxist and Leninist thinking, which clashed with the ideological pretensions of cold war scholars. So it is not a form of analysis that you see taught, for the most part, in U.S. universities today.

Geopolitics was also an ideology in the late nineteenth and early twentieth centuries—a self-conscious set of beliefs on which elites and leaders of the great powers acted. It was the thinking behind the imperialism of that period, the logic for the acquisition of colonies with specific geographical locations. The incidents leading up to the First World War came out of this mode of thinking, such as the 1898 Fashoda incident over the headwaters of the Nile River that gave rise to a near conflict between Third Republic France and late-Victorian Britain.

In the case of the United States, it became the dominant mode of thinking at the time of Teddy Roosevelt and led to the decision by Roosevelt and his cabal of associates to turn the United States into an empire. This was a conscious project. It was not an accident. The Spanish- American War was an intentional device by which the United States acquired an empire. The Spanish-American War and the occupation of the Philippines were followed quickly by the seizure of Panama, openly justified by geopolitical ideology. To see just how self-conscious this process was, I recommend Warren Zimmermann's *First Great Triumph.*[1] The parallels to the current moment are striking.

Geopolitical ideology was later appropriated by Hitler and Mussolini and by the Japanese militarists to explain and to justify their expansionist behavior. And it was this expansionist behavior—which threatened the geopolitical interest of the opposing powers—that led to the Second World War, not the internal politics of Germany, Italy, or Japan.

This ideology disappeared to some degree during the cold war in favor of a model of ideological competition. That is to say, geopolitical ideology appeared to be inconsistent with the high-minded justifications (in which "democracy" and "freedom" largely figured) given for interventions in the third world.

But really, if you study the history of the Cold War, the overt conflicts that took place were consciously framed by a geopolitical orientation from the American point of view. The United States had to control the Middle East and its oil. That was the basis of the Truman Doctrine and the Eisenhower Doctrine and the Carter Doctrine. The United States had to control parts of Africa because of its mineral wealth in copper, cobalt, and platinum. That's why the United States backed the apartheid regime in South Africa. And the reason for both the Korean War and the Vietnam War was understood at the highest levels in terms of the U.S. interest in controlling the Pacific Rim.

Today, we are seeing a resurgence of unabashed geopolitical ideology among the leaders of the major powers, above all in the United States. In fact, the best way to see what's happening today in Iraq and elsewhere is through a geopolitical prism. American leaders have embarked on the classical geopolitical project of assuring U.S. dominance of the most important resource areas, understood as the sources of power and wealth. There is an ideological consistency to what they're doing, and it is this geopolitical mode of thinking.

Perhaps there is some question as to exactly how conscious this is, but you can see this way of thinking in the overt discourse of many contemporary leaders. Dick Cheney and some prominent neoconservatives especially, but also Democrats such as Zbigniew Brzezinski, speak in this manner. They openly state that the United States is engaged in a struggle to maintain its power vis-a-vis other contending great powers and that America must prevail.

Now, you might ask, what contending great powers? It might seem far from obvious that any exist. But if you read what these folks write and hear what they say, you will find that they are absolutely obsessed by the potential emergence of rival great powers: Russia, China, a European combination of some sort, Japan, and even India.

This is the essence of the Wolfowitz Doctrine, first articulated in the Pentagon's *Defense Planning Guidance* document for 1994–1999, first leaked to the press in February 1992. This document calls for proactive U.S. military intervention to deter and prevent the rise of a contending competitor and asserts that the United States must use any and all means necessary to prevent that from happening. At the time, this doctrine was met with such howls of outrage from U.S. allies that then President Bush had to squelch the document, and it was revised to take out the offending language.

But the doctrine lingered in the think-tank writings of the 1990s, reemerging as the official global military policy of the Bush II administration. It has now been incorporated as the core principle of the document known as the *National Security Strategy of the United States of America* (September 2002), available for download from the White House website.[2] This document states explicitly that the ultimate purpose of American power is to prevent the rise of a competing great power, and that the United States shall use any means necessary to prevent that from happening, including preventive military force when needed, but also through spending so much money on defense that no peer competitor can ever arise.

Against this background, it can hardly be questioned that the purpose of the war in Iraq is to redraw the geopolitical map of Eurasia to insure and embed U.S. power and dominance in the region vis-a-vis these other potential competitors.

Now let us step back for a minute and return to the classical geopolitical thinking of the early part of the last century, particularly the views of Sir Halford Mackinder of Great Britain. He held that Eurasia was the most important part—the "heartland"—of the civilized world, and that whoever controlled this heartland by definition controlled the rest of the world because of the concentration there of population, resources, and industrial might. In classical geopolitical thinking, world politics is essentially a struggle over control of the Eurasian heartland.

The strategists of the turn of the twentieth century saw two ways through which global dominance could arise. One was through the emergence of a continental power (or a combination of continental powers) that dominated Eurasia and was, therefore, the master of the world. It was precisely this fear—that a German-controlled continental Europe and Russia, together with a Japanese-dominated China and Southeast Asia, would merge into a vast continental power and dominate the Eurasian heartland, thereby reducing the United States to a marginal power—which galvanized American leaders at the onset of the Second World War. Franklin D. Roosevelt was deeply steeped in this mode of analysis, and it is this ideological-strategic view that triggered U.S. intervention in the Second World War.

The other approach to global dominance perceived by early twentieth century geopolitical strategists was to control the "rimlands" of Eurasia—that is, Western Europe, the Pacific Rim, and the Middle East—and thereby contain any emerging "heartland" power. After the Second World War, the United States determined that it would in fact maintain a permanent military presence in all of the rimlands of Eurasia. This is what we know as the "containment" strategy. And it was this outlook that led to the formation of NATO, the Marshall Plan, SEATO, CENTO, and the U.S. military alliances with Japan and Taiwan. For most of the time since the Second World War, the focus has been on the eastern and western ends of Eurasia—Europe and the Far East.

What is happening now, I believe, is that U.S. elites have concluded that the European and East Asian rimlands of Eurasia are securely in American hands or less important, or both. The new center of geopolitical competition, as they see it, is south-central Eurasia, encompassing the Persian Gulf area, which possesses two-thirds of the world's oil, the Caspian Sea basin, which has a large chunk of what's left, and the surrounding countries of Central Asia. This is the new center of world struggle and conflict, and the Bush administration is determined that the United States shall dominate and control this critical area.

Until now, the contested rimlands of Eurasia were the base of U.S. power, while in the south-central region there was but a very modest presence of U.S. forces. Since the end of the Cold War, however, the primary U.S. military realignment has entailed the drawdown of American forces in East Asia and Europe along with the buildup of forces in the south-central region. U.S. bases in Europe are being closed, while new military bases are being established in the Persian Gulf area and in Central Asia.

It is important to note that this is a process that began *before* 9/11. September 11 quickened the process and gave it a popular mandate, but this was entirely serendipitous from the point of view of U.S. strategists. It was President Clinton who initiated U.S. military ties with Kazakhstan, Uzbekistan, Georgia, and Azerbaijan, and who built up the U.S. capacity to intervene in the Persian Gulf–Caspian Sea area. The U.S. invasion of Iraq was not a victory of Wolfowitz and Rumsfeld; it was Clinton's work that made this victory possible.

The war against Iraq was intended to provide the United States with a dominant position in the Persian Gulf region and to serve as a springboard for further conquests and assertion of power in the region. It was aimed as much, if not more, at China, Russia, and Europe as at Syria or Iran. It is part of a larger process of asserting dominant U.S. power in south-central Eurasia, in the very heartland of this mega-continent.

But why specifically the Persian Gulf/Caspian Sea area, and why now? In part, because this is where most of the world's remaining oil is located—approximately 70 percent of known petroleum reserves. And you have to think of oil not just as a source of fuel—although that's very important—but as a source of power. As U.S. strategists see it, whoever controls Persian Gulf oil controls the world's economy and, therefore, has the ultimate lever over all competing powers.

In September 1990, then secretary of defense Dick Cheney told the Senate Armed Services Committee that Saddam Hussein would acquire a "stranglehold" over the U.S. and world economy if he captured Saudi Arabia's oilfields along with those of Kuwait. This was the main reason, he testified, why the United States must send troops to the area and repel Hussein's forces. He used much the same language in a speech last August to the Veterans of Foreign Wars. I believe that in his mind it is clear that the United States must retain a stranglehold on the world economy by controlling this area. This is just as important, in the administration's view, as retaining the U.S. advantage in military technology.

Ten years from now, China is expected to be totally dependent on the Persian Gulf and the Caspian Sea area for the oil it will need to sustain its economic growth. Europe, Japan, and South Korea will be in much the same position. Control over the oil spigot may be a somewhat cartoonish image, but it is an image that has motivated U.S. policy since the end of the Cold War and has gained even more prominence during the Bush-Cheney administration.

This region is also the *only* area in the world where the interests of the putative great powers collide. In the hotly contested Caspian Sea area, Russia is an expanding power, China is an expanding power, and the United

States is an expanding power. There is no other place in the world like this. They are struggling with one another consciously and actively. The Bush administration is determined to dominate this area and to subordinate these two potential challengers and prevent them from forming a common front against the United States.[3]

What then are the implications of this great realignment of U.S. geopolitical strategy made possible by the cold war defeat of the Soviet Union?

It is much too early to draw any definitive conclusions, but some things can be said. First, Iraq is just the beginning of a U.S. drive into this area. We will see further extensions and expressions of U.S. power in the region. This will provoke resistance and conscious opposition to the United States by insurgent groups and regimes. But the United States will also become enmeshed in local conflicts that arose long before its involvement in the region. For example, the conflict between Armenia and Azerbaijan, and that between Abkhazia and Georgia—both of which have a long history—will impact U.S. security as the United States becomes dependent on a newly constructed trans-Caucasus oil pipeline. The Chechen and Afghan wars continue and bracket the region. In all such disputes there is a likelihood of indirect or direct, covert or overt intervention by the United States and the other contending powers.

We are at the beginning, I believe, of a new cold war in south-central Eurasia, with many possibilities for crises and flare-ups, because nowhere else in the world are Russia and China directly involved and supporting groups and regimes that are opposed to the United States. Even during the height of the cold war, there wasn't anything quite comparable to this. American troops will be there for a long time, with a high risk of violent engagement and the potential for great human suffering. It appears, then, that the U.S. and international peace movement will have a lot of work ahead!

6

U.S. Hegemony Today

PETER GOWAN

American hegemony since 1945 has been structurally different in its degree and type of dominance from that of any other power in the history of capitalism. Instead of simply being the biggest power with the biggest capitalist economy among a number of great powers, the United States was able to exercise political dominance over the entire capitalist core. Before 1945 different capitalist centers had different geographic zones of political and economic dominance. The United States ended that arrangement, making the whole capitalist world its geographic sphere of political dominance. On this basis it shaped and reshaped the conditions and forms of international capital accumulation throughout the capitalist world.

The question today is whether the United States can continue this system in the post-cold war world. This is the question that has been obsessing American and other state leaders since 1989, and it is the governing item on the agenda of the Bush administration just as it was on the agenda of the Clinton administration. As the Bush Senior administration noted correctly in its 1992 draft *Defense Planning Guidance*, the key threat to this kind of American hegemony lies in regionalist political challenges from the two other main centers of core capitalism: those at the western and at the eastern ends of Eurasia. The U.S. grand strategy since the collapse of the Soviet bloc has sought to ensure that such regionalist political developments do not force the United States into accepting a more collegial political center of world capitalism.

The resulting conflicts and aggressive power plays by the United States are thus focused today principally upon competition between capitalist centers, not direct conflicts between the United States and international labor and the anti-imperialist left. This article attempts to explore the forms and substance of intercapitalist relations in the post-1945 era of American hegemony.

AMERICAN HEGEMONISM: THE COLD WAR HUB-AND-SPOKES MODEL

American hegemonism during the cold war was widely seen, on the left as well as on the right, as really nothing more than U.S. leadership of a core capitalist *partnership*. In other words, the core capitalist states were seen as having established a deep, organic, cooperative alliance to defeat Communism, manage international capital accumulation, and keep the South open and under control. In this view, the United States was simply the first among equals, enjoying that status because of its size. Marxists had a model for this: a Kautskyite "ultra-imperialism." And this vision was even radicalized in the 1990s into conceptions of a transnational capitalist class across the core, with a shared identity and shared fundamental interests to match. But this view is not, and has never been, an accurate reflection of reality.

There was indeed a partnership of core capitalist states during the cold war in the fight against Communism and to keep the South under control. This partnership was embodied in institutions like the international financial institutions, the General Agreement on Tariffs and Trade (GATT), and the security alliances, as well as Western cooperation in the United Nations.

But there was not only partnership. There was also U.S. political dominance over the other core states. The partnership and its institutional expressions could be thought of as a superstructure. But underpinning that superstructure was a deeper structure of American political dominance.

This deep structure derived from the ability of the United States to create a particular kind of hub-and-spokes structure of relations which ensured that each of the core capitalist states' political relationship with the U.S. hub was more crucial to its vital interests than any other possible relationship with any other power.

During the cold war this hub-and-spokes arrangement of dependency operated as a *political system,* which continually reproduced itself. This system was constructed in the second half of the 1940s when all the main capitalist centers in Eurasia were desperately dependent upon the United States in almost every field: West Germany and Japan were occupied by the United States; the capitalist classes of France and Italy were weak and threatened internally, while the French state was desperate for help to regain and retain its empire and was also worried about a German revival; Britain was financially crippled and desperate for resources to retain its empire. All needed dollars and American imports.

In these conditions the U.S. ruling elites, under the guidance of Dean Acheson, hit upon a masterly concept for assuring long-term American political dominance over the entire core. It offered to help all the main capitalist states with each of their key concerns, whether imperial or for reintegration into the state system, or fear of each other, or in some cases fear of domestic Communism. But at the same time, it asked them to join U.S.-centered alliances for a military confrontation with the Soviet bloc and Communism.

Once the other powers had accepted the *governing* character of the global cleavage between the "free world" and the "Communist enemy," overriding all other possible political cleavages, the United States swiftly made that cleavage the basis for a continuous military confrontation with the Communist world. And it also drove the cleavage into the domestic political systems of the allies: the basis upon which a party was to be treated as legitimate within these domestic political systems was where it stood on the global divide.

In the generalized military confrontation with the Soviet Union, the United States became the protector power, since if a war broke out between the United States and the Soviet Union, the allies of the United States lacked the military capacity to defend their territories from Soviet conventional forces. The United States thus acquired the rights of such a protector power: a substantial degree of control and supervision of each ally's military and foreign policy strategies, as well as an insistence on an overriding allegiance to their relationship with the United States, not to be substituted by any other alliance relationship. In return for guaranteeing their security, the United States could ask for special rights and privileges in both the political and the economic field. The result was a unipolar capitalist world in which the United States had the right to take unilateral decisions on the great global cleavage with the Communist bloc.

This set of political relationships at an interstate level was then buttressed by the structure of the allies' domestic political systems. These effectively precluded the possibility of legitimate political leaderships emerging on an international line of opposition to the global politics of the United States.

A further beauty of this system was that it provided the basis for rebuilding aggressive bourgeois parties within the allied states. Such parties could trump parties of labor and the left by being the most aggressive anti-Soviet and anti-Communist political force. And they could use the military threat and the ideological connection between social democrats and Communists as weapons against domestic demands for social reform. Thus the interests of domestic capitalist power and strong pro-Americanism became virtually synonymous in most allied states.

The one weak center in this system was French Gaullism, for long the main political force on the right in France and a nationalist force rather than a cold war pro-American force. De Gaulle withdrew from the military structure of NATO and removed U.S. troops from France, while simultaneously taking strong stands against some U.S. political drives in the South. But France did not leave the alliance itself and was in most respects still strongly linked to the United States in East-West relations. French attempts in the early 1960s to form a bloc with Germany and the attempt of the West Europeans to form a common position on Israeli-Arab relations in the early 1970s were both easily defeated.

This set of dependencies was supplemented by others as the West European empires crumbled. The core states found that their links to oil and raw material suppliers in the South and the protection of their investments in the South depended increasingly on American power and operations in the South. If the United States imposed sanctions on, say, an important supplier of oil, the core state which had been buying that oil or whose company was extracting it would be suddenly cut off. And if a revolution or coup d'état threatened the foreign investments of any core capitalism, crushing the challenge would typically require either direct help from the United States or its acquiescence.

The U.S. role as leader of the core in controlling the South was weakened by its defeat in Vietnam, but it managed to use proxy forces along with its sea and air power and capacity for covert action to sustain this system. It is worth stressing that this set of cold war arrangements was not some sort of trick or bluff. There was a genuine cold war confrontation and it did, on the whole, serve the interests of all the core capitalist states very well. There was bound to be a degree of conflict between the Soviet Union and the capitalist world and there was bound to be deep hostility between Communist Parties and the various capitalist classes where Communism was a threat. But these antipathies did not necessarily lead to a massive expansion of American power into Eurasia, turning the rest of the core capitalist states into subaltern allies. This was the achievement of the Achesonian system.

DEVELOPMENT PATHS FOR OTHER CAPITALIST STATES BUT DOMINANCE FOR U.S. CAPITALISM

This political system was a necessary but not a sufficient condition for sustained U.S. hegemony over the capitalist core. Sustained hegemony required that the United States could offer a development path for other core capitalist classes while at the same time structuring the patterns of international capital accumulation in ways that facilitated a leading position for American capitalism.

A development path is not just about economics. It is also about politics. Capitalist classes must be confident that they have a secure path toward their own enrichment—an effective way of extracting value out of production activity. They must also have a path to the strengthening of the political authority of their state over their population: economics and politics must combine in what is at bottom an overall social power strategy of development.

But there is an obvious tension between providing a development path for other core capitalisms and assuring the continued dominance of American capitalism. For thirty years the United States triumphantly achieved this task, but its efforts to restructure patterns of accumulation from the 1970s on were fraught with tensions and problems.

In the first phase of the postwar period, war destruction and economic dislocation in Eurasia offered the possibility of a great postwar reconstruction boom. And American capitalism was the bearer of a new type of industrial capitalism with very dynamic possibilities. The so- called Fordist type of capitalism was different from the typical interwar and nineteenth-century European form of capitalism. This had involved using workers only for production, while the products of the most advanced industries were to be sold to middle-class markets around the world. The Fordist idea gave the industrial workers the possibility of a role also in "realization," as consumers of the products of advanced industries. And when this idea was linked to the power of the labor movements, often Communist led, that emerged in a number of West European societies after the Second World War, and was linked also to Keynesian ideas of class compromise in economics and to fears of Communism, the basis was laid for a powerful economic growth dynamic in Western Europe based upon a great deepening of domestic product markets.[1]

These production arrangements were sufficiently dynamic to draw the social democratic labor movements into stable cooperation with the new social order, giving the states concerned a solid basis for establishing liberal democracy. In societies where this class coalition was too shaky, the United States backed authoritarian regimes, as in the Mediterranean European states (with Italy as a halfway house) and in South Korea and Taiwan.

Fitting these development paths together with the dominance of American capitalism was relatively easy in the 1947–1970 period. On the one hand, U.S. planners took the strategic decision to revive both German and Japanese capitalisms as the industrial hubs of their respective regions. These centers were thus destined to become the main competitors of American capitalism in the central field of industrial production. But at the same time, they were also the most strongly controlled and dependent in the political field, as quasi-protectorates, and were thus most susceptible to U.S. political pressure.

For twenty years Washington's strategy for assuring the dominance of U.S. capitalism was centered on opening European labor markets to U.S. capital and opening product markets to U.S. industrial goods. On one side, Washington's 1954 economic agreement with Germany guaranteed that German product and labor markets would be open to U.S. products and foreign direct investments. On the other side, Washington pushed for a treaty-based West European integration which would guarantee in international law the openness of each West European economy to the products of other West European economies. Thus, from their West German base, American industrial capitals would have access to the product markets of the whole of Western Europe.

The result was a single unified political and economic space covering the entire capitalist core under U.S. political and economic leadership. On this basis, the United States and other core states could act in partnership to control the South.

THE 1970S CRUNCH AND THE DRIVE FOR NEW DEVELOPMENT PATHS FAVORING U.S. ASCENDANCY

By the 1970s, the United States faced a powerful competitive challenge from the industrial capitalisms of Germany and Japan. And the Fordist path had produced an industrial labor movement with great social power and a large measure of entrenched security. The result was a crisis of core-wide development strategy. The old strategy could have been continued, but it would have involved a deepening of collegial management of international economics, a deeper corporatist collaboration with labor, and a more inclusive arrangement with the South. Some capitalist groups argued for this in the 1970s, as in the Brandt Commission. But victory was achieved by the Anglo-American New Right's program.

This involved a rollback of the social power of labor in the core countries, a rollback of the social coalitions for state-centered development in the South, and a return to the forms of capitalism that had existed in the pre-1945 period and before the New Deal. Post-1945 restrictions on the property rights of capital were to be swept away: capital would no longer be treated as an instrument for achieving social goals such as full employment and social welfare; it would be treated as king. State social policy would be governed by the priority of serving capital in all fields. And capital would no longer mean industrial output: it would mean money capital, the largest possible pyramids of finance, looking for the most profitable rate of return in any direction at home and abroad. Tightly parcelized and controlled credit systems were to be swept away; controls on the right to move financial property in any direction were to be abolished; public services and state industrial sectors were to be offered to money capital; macroeconomic policy was to be geared to protecting the value of money capital; and fiscal policy was to be geared to freeing money capital from taxation. This was a program for a return to the late- nineteenth-century capitalism of J. P. Morgan or Barings. Labor was to be shoved out the door again, allowed only to press its collective nose against the icy window to gaze at the feasting financial barons and their political toadies within. Keynes was dead and the rentiers were back, waving books by Hayek and hailing the new road from the supposed postwar serfdom of capital.[2]

But linked to this recidivist program for social change within capitalist societies was also a new set of inflections of the effort to maintain the dominance of American capitalism. To understand this we must first examine how the United States sought to structure the international political economy in the postwar period to combine development paths for all with the ascendancy of U.S. capitalism.

THE AMERICAN PLAYING FIELD FOR INTERNATIONAL CAPITALISM

The ideology of the postwar international economy was free trade on a multilateral basis. The idea was that international economics within the capitalist world was radically separated from politics and the international economy was based not only on common rules applicable to all, but on rules that were derived from the norms and principles of free trade, enabling comparative advantage to drive the international division of labor for the benefit of all.

But the United States never really had a free trade approach to international economics, nor a multilateralist approach. The basic tradition was to open others' markets to whatever sectors U.S. business was strongest in, while protecting U.S. sectors which faced superior competitors. The U.S. principle was reciprocity rather than most-favored-nation multilateralism. And this tradition persisted throughout the postwar period.

At the same time, these policies were partly concealed by other features of the American approach: U.S. postwar expansion was led less by trade than by foreign direct investment—a pattern that has persisted to the present day. Sales revenues from American overseas subsidiaries have been, and remain, far larger than U.S. export revenues. Thus for the most dynamic and internationalized sectors of U.S. business, the key issues were not so much tariffs and quotas and safeguards—the traditional stuff of trade politics—but access to labor markets abroad for U.S. capitals under very favorable terms. Thus the United States ensured, when the European Economic Community was created, that it would treat U.S. capitals (unlike other foreign capitals) as if they were European, with full "national treatment." Secondly, the United States did allow international economics to be governed by legal procedural rules to a great extent. It did not, on the whole, support managed trade geared to volume targets. Formally, the United States remained outside the GATT regime—the U.S. Senate never ratified GATT. But it allowed the GATT system to work in a legal sense, by and large.

The fact that international economic exchanges were largely governed by legal procedural rules was important because it gave capitalists everywhere a large measure of predictability and security for their operations. But the legal rules themselves were "positive law," not norm-based on liberal free trade principles. The world of international trade law thus became a thicket of power-driven interests in which arguments were won less by those on the side of the angels of liberalism than by those able to pay the biggest lawyers' fees and able to use market power threats to settle arguments about trade rights.

Against this background we can note the ways in which the United States sought to maintain its capitalism's dominance on an international level. The general goal has been to assure U.S. leadership in new growth sectors and to ensure U.S. entry into (and supervision of) new growth centers. New growth sectors are in the so-called high-tech fields, especially technologies with a wide impact across economies. New growth centers are those countries or regions experiencing rapid, sustained economic growth; such centers need to be both penetrated by U.S. capitals and brought under U.S. political dominance so that the United States can have leverage over their future development path.

Very important in ensuring leadership in new growth sectors is American industrial policy, and not least the role of the military budget in such policy. This can fund research and development which can generate new growth technologies. It can also prime the pump with large military-related investments in relevant infrastructure and with the U.S. state acting as an initial market for the products. No other core capitalist country has an equivalent set of instruments for launching new growth sector technologies.

When U.S. fears arise that another center may be developing new growth sectors of global reach, it is inclined to sweep aside the liberal rhetoric and demand managed trade, using political threats. The classic example here was its confrontations with Japan in the late 1980s and early 1990s over microchips and semiconductors; here the United States simply imposed a bilateral managed trade regime.

As for new growth centers, the U.S. attitude to exclusion has again been demonstrated by the example of Japan in the 1980s and also other East and Southeast Asian countries in the 1990s, with America's insistent pressure for opening up to the entry of U.S. capitals: the classic example here is the U.S. Department of the Treasury's operations toward South Korea in 1997–1998. And for a new growth center such as China, the drive to assure a liberal political regime easily influenced by U.S. leverage is evident today. A key lever for exerting pressure on new growth centers is that of opening the U.S. market to their products in exchange for their opening their asset and other markets to the entry of U.S. capitals.

But the recidivist turn to private finance-centered capitalism in the United States and its U.K. satellite was combined with an important new range of instruments for assuring the dominance of U.S. capitalism. The most important of these is what I have called elsewhere the Dollar Wall Street Regime (DWSR).[3]

THE IMPERIAL MONETARY SHIFT AND THE DOLLAR WALL STREET REGIME

The concept of a free-trade level playing field in international economics has been premised on the assumption of a homogeneous, stable international monetary system. Multilateral steps eliminating trade barriers will not create a level playing field if a leading state can then manipulate exchange rates at will and free itself from the payments discipline that applies to other states. And when that leading state is also the producer of the world's main international currency, you have something like an imperial economic framework facing other capitalisms. You also have a monetary framework constantly generating payments crises and debt crises all over the place—except in the state issuing the lead currency. That is why, from the nineteenth century until the early 1970s, all authorities accepted the need for a stable, homogeneous international monetary order. But then the American authorities broke with that tradition and turned in just such an imperial direction.

The first step was taken with the closing of the Gold Window in August 1971—a conscious strategic decision, planned far in advance, entailing a conscious rejection of a new, reformed homogeneous international monetary order.[4] This was followed by the effective sabotage by the United States of attempts by the rest of the capitalist states to construct a new system in the early 1970s.[5] And after an agreement to manage the dollar exchange rate with the deutsche mark and the yen at the Rambouillet Summit of 1975, the United States in fact soon went its own way, eventually dismissing the whole idea of such management in the early Reagan years.

The result has been quasi-imperial in two main respects. First, by fragmenting the international monetary system, it pushes economic operators and states to seek stability by operating almost entirely within what is in effect a dollar bloc. For them, the only alternative to extreme monetary instability is to regionalize their operations behind a monetary shield of their own, as the West Europeans chose to do beginning with the de facto construction of the deutsche mark bloc in 1979.

Second, by freeing the dollar from the constraints of any international anchor and rules common to all, the United States could unilaterally subordinate international monetary conditions to the perceived requirements of American capitalism. When the United States was in recession, the U.S. authorities could drive the dollar down to generate an export-led revival; when the United States was rising into boom, the Treasury Department could swing the dollar up massively against other currencies.

Some believe that these gigantic swings in exchange rates are steered not by governments but by financial markets and foreign exchange markets. This is superficially true but actually false. These markets are situated principally in New York and its London satellite. The biggest players in these markets take their cue in exchange rate issues from every word and gesture of the Treasury Department's authorities and every move by the authorities of the Federal Reserve Bank of New York. And since the two sides share fundamentally common interests, the U.S. Treasury Department can use the main financial market operators precisely as instruments and multipliers of public policy.[6]

The full force of this power to swing the dollar's value in great arcs can be appreciated when we remember the consequences of the dollar's role as the main monetary unit of account and as the main means of payment for oil and many other international products. However much the dollar swings one way or the other, prices do not change for these products for those operating in the dollar zone. Furthermore, because of the dollar's dominance as a means of payment, the United States can run up huge current account deficits and enormous external debts without facing the kind of monetary payments constraints facing other states.

The dominance of the dollar is not simply the result of the size of the U.S. economy. It is also and importantly the result of two other things: politics and finance. A state that protects regimes and trade routes all over the world can, as Britain showed with its sterling area, gain the privileges of having a world money. So can the United States. A state that controls the sources of world oil politically can ensure that oil is priced and largely paid for in its currency—in this case, in dollars—and thus can defend its international dominance. And a state which is the most politically secure in the world is a very safe place for storing financial property, thus ensuring huge inflows of funds into financial capital—in this case, New York and its London (offshore) satellite. And a state with the largest, most liquid financial market in the world is the least risky place to store wealth since you can swiftly move your wealth out for other purposes in such large, liquid markets.

The central structure of postwar capitalist economies had been the national columns running from the state through a tightly brigaded financial system to the industrial structures. The Anglo-American return to a Morgan-Barings style financial capitalism placed the private financial pyramids at the heart of the system, the industrial structures taking their places alongside real estate, private housing finance, private health care, and a host of other private services, with the state's role redefined as the protector and service-provider for this new structure.

The rise of the DWSR, assisted by the diplomatic efforts of Washington and London, opened the possibility of a vast new field of expansion outward for American capitalism. Just as New York financial pyramids in the late nineteenth century acquired dominance over industrial capitalism further west by financing its development, so American financial pyramids at the end of the twentieth century could acquire dominance over industrial capitalists across the rest of the core. By sweeping away all restrictions on the centralization of American finance and by drawing Main Street under the sway of Wall Street, the American authorities gave American financial pyramids an overwhelming edge in international finance by the end of the 1980s. With the structural instability in exchange rates, industrial capitals in Europe and in East Asia could not securely expand their sales in the United States through export strategies. They had to expand their operations through mounting production operations in all three centers. And with overcapacity in most established industrial sectors, and the consequent need to rapidly seize international markets with new products, the need to link up with American finance could become overwhelming.

Changes were also sought in the institutional structure of capitalism to ensure that industrial companies were dependent on securities markets and to ensure that hostile takeovers were permitted, with the intent that productive assets across the capitalist world would fall into American ownership and a vast transnational centralization of capital would be possible. And in conditions of generalized capitalist stagnation and crisis in much of the world, paradoxically governments and banks and industrial companies were desperate for American finance to tide them over, giving American finance capitalism ever widening circles of control over international capitalism. International monetary instability greatly enhanced these possibilities.

The drive to transform capitalism across the capitalist world into a new private-finance-centered social system increasingly integrated into an international capitalism dominated by the DWSR has continued for twenty years. It is widely assumed that the entire capitalist core has accepted this drive and changed accordingly. The idea of a globalized economy governed by neoliberalism expresses this assumption. Yet in reality we have seen relations between capitalist centers become much more tension-ridden, *despite the fact that in all centers there has been a drive to shift social power from labor to capital.* The concept of neoliberalism captures the generalized drive against the social power of labor. But it does not capture the parallel tension-ridden relations between the three main centers of capitalism.

Although the West European states and Japan have liberalized financial systems, scrapped capital controls, and accepted the forcing open of other financial systems and service sectors through the Word Trade Organization (WTO) and other mechanisms, neither the West Europeans nor the East Asians have fully embraced the U.S. model and the U.S. program for the world economy. The West Europeans built a regional monetary shield against the dollar system and combined an adaptive deal with the United States on the WTO with efforts greatly to strengthen their own economic and regulatory integration through the European Union (EU). And in East Asia there have been strong reactive tendencies towards regional networks.

Neither in Western Europe nor in East Asia have these defensive reactions been taken on behalf of labor. Far from it. The West European regionalist defense mechanisms have also been mechanisms for eroding the social power of labor, most obviously in the policy framework for the euro, which is patently geared toward driving through a qualitative weakening of the rights and bargaining strength of labor, particularly in Germany.

No other capitalist center has advanced an alternative program for international capital accumulation or proclaimed its own capitalism as an alternative model to that of the United States. Only through the emergence of such an alternative can the advance of the U.S. model be checked or defeated. And indeed, the risks of advancing such an alternative would be very great. It could after all stimulate labor to join the challenge. It could split the capitalist core's approach to the South in political economy matters, opening the way toward resistance to common transatlantic economic interests in the South. And above all it could delegitimize the American model even within the United States itself. These possible consequences ensure that any important center offering an alternative would face ferocious resistance from the United States and its transnational supporters.

The fact that neither the German nor the Japanese capitalist classes and states have embraced the new American system is extremely important and it is all the more remarkable given the gigantic pressures from the 1995–2000 American boom. But the boom has now turned out to have been a bubble, and the American bubble has turned out to have involved a great deal of parasitic and predatory activity, undermining the American productive base, as in the paradigmatic case of Enron. This marks a substantial setback for the drive to reorganize American and international capitalism to assure U.S. capitalist dominance through the first half of the twenty-first century.

NEW CHALLENGES TO AMERICAN HEGEMONY AND U.S. RESPONSES

Against this background we can more easily appreciate the challenges to U.S. hegemony in the post–Cold War period. We will first examine the challenges and then consider the possible strategies of the United States for meeting them.

The Soviet bloc collapse has had a number of negative consequences for the exercise of U.S. political dominance over the capitalist core. The East Asian capitalisms (Japan, South Korea, and Taiwan) remain dependent on U.S. military power for their security, but largely as a result of U.S. policies. This is most obvious in the case of South Korea. If the U.S. were to sign a peace treaty with the North and assure its security, South Korean security dependence on the U.S. would be ended.

But the security dependence of Western Europe on U.S. military capacity ended with the disappearance of the Soviet Union. This has opened up a very considerable threat to America's global political dominance because it has facilitated a turn on the part of West European continental states toward building an increasingly strong political caucus, undermining the hub- and-spokes division and dependency of West European states in the field of international politics.

The West European states did not turn toward stronger political integration out of some collective will to launch a bid for world leadership, supplanting the United States. They did so because of the confluence of a number of specific pressures and needs. Germany desired to bind other West European states more closely around it, worrying that its greatly enhanced power might lead its neighbors (not least France) to want to gang up against it. Since France (and Britain) resisted a decisive move to a federal democratic EU, the alternative was that of a strong political bloc in international politics. These states also perceived the need to present a common political as well as economic front to east Central Europe, and the obvious method for doing so was by strengthening the EU as the political instrument for processing German and other West European policies towards the East.

Critically, the EU was the main instrument for transforming social relations within its member states in a "neoliberal" direction. The basic idea was to use European social democratic enthusiasm for European unity against European social democratic commitment to labor rights. But in the 1990s, the European economies were stagnating with high unemployment and the EU lacked any genuine democratic legitimacy. Therefore, to enhance the authority of the EU in pursuit of neoliberalism, new policy areas and activities were sought which would appeal to the European center-left. Many of these were in the international political field: campaigns on human rights, environmentalism, arms control, aid, and a host of other such causes. No longer legitimating the EU as a social model for the world, the EU states sought to legitimate it as the supreme global champion of the pacification of the world through international law rather than through power politics.

The drive for monetary union and the establishment of the euro was perceived, rightly, in continental Western Europe as requiring a greatly strengthened political base; but gaining such a base was very difficult, especially because of the continued divisions within French state elites on French national strategy. What could be called a Mitterrandist wing was committed to France as a regionalist power, focused on leading Western Europe through the EU—a national strategy requiring very close collaboration with Germany, but the other wing, which could be called the Chirac tendency, defined French national strategy in terms of France being a small global power, with its bomb and seat on the U.N. Security Council. And as for the British role, it was principally directed to being the champion in the EU of the Anglo-American model of private- finance-centered capitalism and to trying to break up the political cohesion of the EU.

But from an American grand-strategy perspective, the erosion of the hub-and-spokes dependency in Europe and the pressures in Western Europe toward political unity constituted a fundamental medium-term threat to American global hegemony. The possibility of an equally large political, financial, and industrial center in Europe could not possibly be anything other than a fundamental power threat. But it was one that could not be acknowledged because since 1947, the United States had itself championed European integration. And although that policy had become increasingly one of words rather than deeds, by the 1980s the bulk of the European intelligentsia and, it seems, much of the political elites did not grasp just what a threat they posed to the United States: a threat equivalent to China, Japan, and South Korea getting together as an East Asian union modeled on the EU, and a threat all the more insidious for being difficult to denounce publicly.

The problem posed by the EU was also connected to the drive for consolidation of the new Anglo-American program for a world of private-finance-centered capitalism, led by an imperial dollar and centered in the American financial pyramids. If the euro was consolidated and euroland were to build a genuinely unified financial base, the pressures toward federal political unity would be very strong, and within such a federal Europe pressures for a kind of capitalist society different from the Anglo-American model would also become very strong. The fact that the huge range of U.S. subsidiaries in the EU—half of all U.S. affiliate business sales abroad are in the EU—benefited greatly from the EU political economy structures (including the euro) made this threat to the United States all the more insidious.

A further threat arose from the possibility that Western Europe could find increasing common ground with East Asia on a wide range of issues in the international political economy: a common hostility to the imperial dollar and the potentially lethal financial strikes by U.S. operators (despite the fact that West European operators had also participated in the operations of U.S. banks and the U.S. Treasury in the East Asian crisis).

The ideological basis for the projection of American military power during the Cold War had been the supposed massive military threat from the Soviet bloc and Communism. This was largely accepted as legitimating the aggressive use of military coercion against pro-Soviet forces and regimes. But with the end of the Cold War, the aggressive use of U.S. military power faced serious legitimation problems. Many voices were raised for military aggression to be outlawed unless it was expressly sanctioned by the Security Council, as laid down in the U.N. Charter. And West European governments supported this line. Attempts by the Clinton administration to identify a new string of enemies—the so-called rogue states, dubbed such in 1994—were branded by many, including European governments, as exaggerated and inappropriate, and efforts by the U.S. government to enforce sanctions against Iran and Libya as well as Cuba were flouted by U.S. allies in Western Europe while the blockade against Iraq was also challenged.

This West European effort to place political-legal constraints on the U.S. use of its major political instrument—its capacity for military aggression—contained the seeds of a new-world- order concept which was potentially very attractive to other capitalist states but thoroughly subversive of the entire way in which the American state is configured. The West European idea, expressed most cogently by German policy elites, is that the Atlantic world should dominate the rest of the world by means of international public law. The Atlantic states, following the example of West European integration, should voluntarily subordinate themselves to international legal rules constraining their sovereign autonomy. They should then ask others wishing access to their markets and close political relations to subordinate themselves to the same rules. And states which egregiously flout the norms supposedly underlying the rules of the international system should then be subject to coercive sanctions, including, but only as a final resort approved by the Security Council, military force. The imperial secret of the whole concept lies in who writes the rules. If they are written by the Atlantic states, they can dress them up as being universalist- liberal, norm-based rules, while in reality they are simply "positive law" rules serving the interests of the Atlantic states. The model here is, of course, the European-inspired WTO which presents its rules as rooted in universalist-liberal free trade norms while in fact they are a concoction of positive-law rules serving Atlantic capitalist interests. Under this world-order concept, military coercive power operates not in opposition to international law but as its enforcer.

Yet the United States has no tradition of subordinating itself to international treaty-based law, and it has no interest in a world order in which military force becomes operational only as a last resort. Yet the West European idea attracts powerful support from other core capitalist states as well as from many states in the South. Such support is indicated by the EU's success, in the face of U.S. opposition, on issues such as the International Criminal Court and the Kyoto Protocols.

These problems contributed to new potential challenges within the United States itself. While the U.S. capitalist class and its political leaders were overwhelmingly committed to maintaining and extending U.S. political dominance and the continued expansion of U.S. capitals on a global scale, the end of the Cold War raised the threat of the U.S. electorate demanding that U.S. government reallocate resources from the military field and overseas expansion to tackling problems at home. Though committed to rebuilding U.S. global political dominance, the Clinton administration did not attempt to mobilize a broad popular constituency for power projection abroad. The boom of the second half of the 1990s eased this potential pressure but did not solve the basic political problem, which had been demonstrated so strongly by the eviction of Bush Senior from the White House despite his Gulf War victory.

We should add the fundamental geopolitical problem inherent in the turns of Russia and China toward capitalism. These turns undermined their useful status as potential threats to a Western Europe and Japan in need of U.S. military services for protection. They also set up competitive pressures within the core countries to gain privileged relations with these two states and privileged access to their labor and product markets and resources and assets. The danger from an American point of view was that in the West a Germany anchored within a more cohesive EU could establish a privileged partnership with Russia, while some or all of the East Asian capitalisms could link up with China in a strong regional network that could weaken American leverage and economic penetration.

A final consequence of the Soviet bloc collapse for American political leverage was the following paradox: America was the purest of symbols of capitalism and thus the defeat of Communism should have greatly enhanced, and in many ways did enhance, the attractive power of the American capitalist model. Yet at the same time, the deepest source of American political power during the postwar period lay in the fact that capitalist classes throughout the world knew that they could rely upon the United States to help crush labor or socialist challenges to their power. With the great decline of this threat after the Soviet collapse, this particular American service was facing significant redundancy. Indeed, there was a growing tendency for liberals and others in the core capitalist countries to argue that the greatest challenge to the world came not from the enemies of liberalism and democracy but from the deep and growing divide between North and South as well as from environmental crises. And on this agenda the United States was identified as a major source of problems rather than as a provider of solutions. And as the 1990s wore on, the pernicious, destructive consequences of the

DWSR and of the WTO regimes generated a growing opposition from young people in the North and from social movements in the South.

Thus, by the end of the 1990s there were plentiful indications that the United States was facing multiple challenges as a result of the Soviet bloc collapse and its consequences. The most serious of these challenges came from what for many was a surprising quarter: Western Europe.

THE BUSH-LIEBERMAN COUNTERPUNCH

There is abundant evidence that in the face of the challenges of the Soviet bloc collapse a consensus quickly emerged in the United States for the American state to attempt to expand its political hegemony from one over the capitalist core to one over the globe as a whole.[7] Ways would be found to bind all the main powers across Eurasia into hub-and-spokes dependency relations with the U.S. of a kind that would ensure that each such power would privilege U.S. political thrusts over all other options.

The Clinton administration emphasized economic statecraft and driving through the program for a new global accumulation regime in which U.S. rentier-centered capitalism would be central. "Economic globalization" and the operations of the U.S. Treasury were at the heart of the Clinton approach on a global scale. At the same time, in the political field, the priority was to reestablish U.S. dominance over Western Europe and over its expansion eastward. The Clinton administration, building on Bush Senior's success in keeping Germany in NATO and thus preserving the NATO structure, successfully undermined West European attempts to resolve the Yugoslav crisis outside the NATO framework. Its Bosnia victory over West European efforts to resolve the crisis was followed by NATO's eastward expansion, a polarization against Russia in the Kosovo War, and the consolidation of strong American political ties with Poland, the Baltic states, Bulgaria, and Romania. But the Clinton administration failed to prevent Western Europe's continuing efforts to strengthen its political cohesion, its search for greater autonomy, and its drive to restrict the political value of U.S. military power.

The West European states responded to U.S. geopolitical maneuvers in Europe by what could be called subversive bandwagoning. They went along with each U.S. thrust, on Bosnia, in the Yugoslav war, and vis-à-vis Russia and NATO enlargement, but they responded simultaneously by trying to strengthen their own regional political unity, most notably in the case of the European Security and Defense Policy, but in other areas as well. And the chief strategic problem for the United States was precisely this West European effort at unity and autonomy on international political questions.

The Bush administration came into office determined to crack the Europeanist nut. September 11, 2001, gave it the opportunity. It announced a new strategic doctrine which utterly repudiated the entire Europeanist position on world order. The new strategic doctrine focused on the legitimate use of force, rogue states, and the politics of the Middle East. The Bush administration then called for war against Iraq *as an operationalization of this strategic doctrine.* It turned to the West European states and asked them if they wished to get on the bandwagon this time, adding that they faced only two choices: being for the United States or against it.

Senator Joseph Lieberman and all the other leading Democrats either supported this line or went along with it. Bush was acting firmly within the programmatic and strategic consensus of the American capitalist class since 1990. Cheney is not a marginal figure; he is a central figure among American class political leaders.

The American attack on Iraq had a number of objectives, in the region and on a global scale (including U.S. control of world oil). But among the global targets, ending the growing cohesion and influence of Western Europe was central.

The war has split Western Europe as intended. It has not, however, produced a strategic victory for the United States in its efforts to consolidate the hub-and-spokes-dependencies basis for a unipolar hegemony. That remains a long way off, and the path to it must include not only military-political victories and large geopolitical maneuvers across Eurasia, but also the political consolidation of the recidivist private-finance-centered rentier capitalism and the imperial dollar across the whole capitalist core.

CONCLUSIONS

Postwar American capitalism and the American state were an advance for West European capitalism over what had gone before, in the interwar period. The Europeanist capitalist program for world politics would now be an advance on the American way today, both in the military- political field and to some degree in the social field. Ironically, this is in large part because of the advances made in Western Europe under American and—to be honest about history—Soviet and Communist influence. But we are now in a chaotic world where the American state is probably too weak to win on a global scale, while the West Europeans and East Asians are probably too weak and divided to shift the direction of world politics in a more pacific and socially inclusive direction.

The U.S. drive to remilitarize world politics as the basis for consolidating its global hegemony in the post–Cold War conditions will tend to generate a vast and heterogeneous coalition of opposition across the globe for some time to come. It will also generate great suffering in many parts of the South. At the same time, the new rentier-centered capitalism is a recipe for social regression on a global scale.

A global left, centered on international labor movements, will arise to oppose the American global program. Already many around the world, most of whom are not socialists, reject the U.S. program. They recognize that the real challenge for capitalism is to demonstrate that it can tackle the North-South divide. It is possible to imagine a capitalism that could tackle this divide: the kind of New Deal–Keynesian–social democratic capitalism that accepted the welfare state model after the Second World War. But that capitalism was born under the spur of the challenge from Stalingrad and a gigantic international Communist movement, with an alternative social program. Without that spur today, we have the old story of chaos, wars, imperialist exploitation—all the things that make Hobson's book on the nature of finance capitalism at the start of the twentieth century fresh and topical today.

7

The Global Minotaur

JOSEPH HALEVI and YANIS VAROUFAKIS

It is now common in Europe and Japan to consider the United States the economic model to emulate. With their economies continuing along the road of prolonged stagnation, mainstream commentators in Europe and Japan are busily seeking out the causes of their regions' economic malaise by comparing their microstructures with those of the United States. Even the recent savage downturn in the United States seems unlikely to alter this trend. In Europe, just as in Japan, prestigious commentators incessantly extol America's comparative advantages: the flexibility of its labor market and its individualist entrepreneurial culture. Such narratives have become the foundation of mainstream explanations of the relative dynamism of the U.S. economy, in contrast to the unwieldy miracle economies of yesteryear.

No one, however, seems to be remotely interested in explaining why Japan and Europe have been led to such dire straits by the very features (a regulated labor market and corporatism) which used to be hailed as the hallmarks of their immense economic success in the sixties, seventies, and eighties. It is as if no one recalls how the Japanese and German success stories were scrutinized for decades in U.S. business schools, for clues to what had gone wrong in America. The best analyses we get on this score are a series of mutterings about how the paradigmatic shift caused by new technologies and the "new economy" has condemned the Euro-Japanese corporate model of development to the scrapheap of economic history.

So, we have two questions, first: What happened to turn Germany and Japan from success stories to, putting it impolitely, basket cases? How did the U.S. economy recover from its sluggish performance to regain its competitive edge? Our second question seems utterly unrelated: Why did Germany and France embrace the peace movement before and during the latest Gulf War?

We begin with the premise that neither of these questions can be understood in terms of the mainstream narratives of economics and politics—that the causes of the present situation are to be found neither in the microeconomies of the world's three leading economic zones (the United States, Europe, and Japan) nor in the sphere of political ethics and diplomacy. In the spirit of Harry Magdoff's *Imperialism: From the Colonial Age to the Present*, we suggest instead that useful insights on these important issues can only obtain when we adopt the broader political economy perspective which takes seriously the form of globalization guiding the international economy ever since the United States gained the upper hand and emerged as the dominant force within global capitalism.[1]

A GRAND GLOBAL DESIGN

The United States came out of the Second World War as the major and, with the exception of Switzerland, the only creditor nation. For the first time since the rise of capitalism, all of the world's trade relied on a single currency and was financed from a single epicenter. Recognizing this remarkable opportunity to achieve unhindered dominance (and to challenge the Soviet Union; a noncapitalist entity which, at the time, the best Western economists thought of as a miracle-in-the-making), the United States took upon itself the role of reconstructing the capitalist world. The grandiose project soon acquired two strands.

First, U.S. policy makers were keen to end the dollar's monopoly as the world's single convertible currency. This monopoly was undesirable because a world trade system relying on a single currency (supported by a single real economy which is only a subset of the global economy) is inherently unstable and prone to major upheavals during the unsavory parts of the business cycle. Initially, they toyed with the idea of propping up the pound sterling and using it as a potential shock absorber for the dollar zone. However, with sterling's collapse in 1947, U.S. officials gave up on this idea.

Instead, they favored, supported, and cajoled the rise of two important supporting pillars for the dollar: one in Europe (the deutsche mark) and one in Japan (the yen). The architects of postwar U.S. globalism were three men: Secretary of the Navy James Forrestral, Secretary of State James Byrnes, and George Kennan. In their eyes, extending credit to Europe and Japan was to become a crucial component of U.S. policy as it would enable these two zones to buy technology and energy products, primarily oil, and attract and utilize (often) migrant labor.

The choice of Germany and Japan seemed entirely logical. Both countries had been rendered dependable (thanks to the overwhelming presence of the U.S. military); both featured a solid industrial base with ample human capital; and both offered considerable geostrategic benefits in relation to the Soviet Union. Britain had to experience the Suez Canal trauma (and the undermining of its colonial rule in Cyprus by the CIA) before realizing this turn in U.S. thinking. It was at that point that successive British governments began clutching at straws; namely, the "special relationship," which turned Great Britain into a minor executor of U.S. policy in exchange for privileged access to the U.S. market for British multinationals and the City of London.

Second, the creation of the two non-dollar currency zones was to be underpinned by political measures to ensure the parallel creation of free-trade areas within these zones so as to carve out crucial vital space for the real economies growing around the new currencies. This strand of the project developed quickly into what eventually became the European Union (EU) in Europe. For Japan, Mao's victory limited the application of this principle. Although the yen and the Japanese economy were bolstered inordinately by successive U.S. administrations, the vital space that the yen required in mainland China was effectively denied it. Instead, the wars in Korea and Vietnam surreptitiously engendered an imperfect, yet still significant, zone within which Japanese trade found space to grow for at least forty years.

The postwar reconstruction of the capitalist world, once these two vital zones (Europe and Japan) were set up, was based on the ability of the United States to extend credit and finance, partly through American multinationals, particularly to Europe and to Japan. The main function of this generous credit policy was to allow Europe and Japan to overcome what was then called the "dollar shortage," a problem that was not eliminated until the mid-1950s.

At that point, the United States realized that it was not enough to have stabilized Europe and Japan. Having financed these two zones sufficiently for them to be able to pay for their inputs (through the Marshall Plan in Europe and war financing during the Korean conflict in the case of Japan), the United States felt the need to take action to guarantee low prices and a constant flow of energy and raw material inputs to these two zones. The loss of China, the trials and tribulations of Latin America, the liberation movements in Southeast Asia, the stirrings in Africa—all these developments motivated the United States to take an aggressive stance against liberation movements in the third world, identified with the threat of rising input prices.

In short, the United States took it upon itself to relegate the periphery to the role of supplier of raw materials to Japan and Western Europe, in addition to North America itself. In the process, U.S. multinationals in energy and other mining activities were doing good business. As for the U.S. domestic economy, there were crucial, beneficial aftereffects. During the 1960s, domestic crises were largely averted through three large public expenditure programs. One of these was Lyndon Johnson's Great Society project, but the other two were closely related to U.S. global strategy: the Intercontinental Ballistic Missile program (ICBM) and the Vietnam War. The latter two strengthened U.S. military-industrial corporations and contributed heftily to the development of the aeronautic-computer-electronics complex (ACE), an economic powerhouse largely divorced from the rest of the U.S. economy.

Nevertheless, we shall dare to speculate that, in the mind of U.S. officials, these were merely hugely desirable by-products of their main policy—namely, guaranteeing energy and input supplies at favorable prices for the reconstruction and development of Europe and Japan. The United States did not hesitate to introduce harsh regulations that ultimately discriminated against American multinationals. Their top priority was not to benefit them directly. The primary task of the wars in Korea and Vietnam was to ensure the continuing supply of cheap raw materials to Europe and Japan. The fact that American multinationals benefitted too was a pleasant side effect.

Interestingly, there was another by-product, possibly one that the United States had not intended at the time: the creation, through war financing, of the vital economic space that Japan had been lacking in the Southeast Asian countries and their so-called tiger economies. Without these wars, countries like Korea, Thailand, Malaysia, and Singapore would have remained underdeveloped and the United States would be Japan's only market (taking into account her partial exclusion from European markets, agreed upon by Europe and the United States).

UNINTENDED CONSEQUENCES YIELD A NEW DESIGN

The above thoughts lead to a reassessment of postwar U.S. dominance from the perspective of the U.S. balance of payments in relation to the rest of the world. The starting point was a large-scale, and impressively ambitious, effort to overcome and to supplant the multiple conflicting imperialisms that characterized the world political economy until the Second World War. The all-encompassing destruction that the war brought to Eurasia and Japan allowed the United States to attempt that which had not been attempted before: global domination of capitalist markets.

As argued in the previous section, while seemingly in competition with the United States, the economies of Germany and Japan were aided by the United States for at least thirty-five years, sometimes through painful U.S. sacrifices. Was this a form of internationalist altruism at work? The more one considers the long-term interests of U.S. accumulation, the less credible that explanation seems. At the heart of U.S. thinking was an intense anxiety regarding the inherent instability of a single-currency, single-zone global system. Indeed, nothing concentrated the minds of U.S. policy makers in the 1950s like the memory of 1929 and the ensuing crisis. These same minds saw an interdependent network comprising three industrial-monetary zones, in which the dollar zone would be predominant (reflecting the centrality of American finance and its military assurance of the flow of inputs from the third world), as the optimal design for the rest of the twentieth century and beyond.

In this sense, if our analysis is correct, the notion that European integration sprang out of a European urge to create some bulwark against American dominance appears to be nothing more than the European Union's creation myth. Similarly, the idea that the Japanese economy grew inexorably against the interests of the United States needs serious reexamination.

Economic historians agree (regardless of ideological perspective) that the United States played a central role in supporting the process of European integration and of Japanese export-oriented industrialization (despite the latter's detrimental effects on the U.S. balance of trade).

Of course, this does not mean that American policy makers were either omniscient or omnipotent. Their best-laid plans often led to disaster. But even when they did fail dismally, these failures proved rather creative, in that they brought about developments neither wholly undesirable nor historically insignificant. We have already, for example, argued that the prosecution of the Vietnam War did not go according to plan. However, the silver lining, from the U.S. policy makers' perspective, is visible to anyone who has ever visited Southeast Asia. Thailand, Malaysia, and Singapore grew fast and in a manner that frustrated the pessimism of neo-Marxist critics of the underdevelopment school (who had predicted that no genuine development of third world countries would be possible under U.S.-led monopoly capitalism). However, there is little doubt that these industrial miracles were instigated by U.S. war spending as a consequence of the lengthy, tragic conflict in Indochina. Just as Japan's economy grew on the back of U.S. military spending during the Korean War, the tigers of Southeast Asia were the offspring of enormous investment, paid for from the U.S. military budget, during the Vietnam War.

Similarly, with the oil crisis of the 1970s, things did not go the way the United States had planned. However, while developments did get out of hand, U.S. policy makers managed to snatch an important array of victories from the jaws of catastrophe. To tell this story properly, we need to start again at the Vietnam War. The military spending that was responsible for the development of Southeast Asia into a type of latter-day Japanese vital zone was also responsible for America's gigantic balance-of-payments deficit, a deficit that, besides its local effects in Southeast Asia, provided much of the expansionary boost that brought the prolonged postwar boom (starting with the Korean War).

This balance-of-payments deficit grew beyond any sustainable level, reflecting the extent to which the Vietnam War confounded the U.S. military's best efforts. With the dollar under inordinate pressure, President Richard Nixon was forced to give up on the stable parity of the dollar to gold, as had been determined in the Bretton Woods agreement. Although U.S. policy makers always felt that the United States could afford, as long as it retained its political dominance within the "free world," a sizable balance of payments deficit, the war in Vietnam had taken it deeply into the red. The unexpected successes of Ho Chi Minh might have unintentionally been the cause of the industrialization of Southeast Asia (courtesy of United States war financing). However, the alarms were ringing furiously in Washington, especially in the Treasury Department and the Federal Reserve. From the late sixties onward, the best and brightest U.S. policy makers sought ways and means to address America's balance of payments problem.

As the financial position of the United States was deteriorating, the continuing growth of the two other main capitalist centers (Europe and Japan), while part of the U.S. plan, began to lose its appeal in Washington. The American quagmire in Indochina was giving rise to two antagonistic effects. On the one hand, it was generating the quantitative conditions for global growth, But on the other hand, it was creating acute rivalries between the United States and its two major protégés in the context of the U.S. balance-of-payments deficit and the ensuing pressure on the dollar.

In his 1982 memoir *Years of Upheaval* Henry Kissinger said categorically that the push to increase oil prices came from the United States.[2] It is now well accepted that Kissinger's memoirs impart accurately the manner in which U.S. decision makers seized upon the OPEC-imposed embargo to push for a sharp increase in oil prices, well beyond what OPEC had planned. The aim was to redress the balance-of-payments situation between the three major zones: the United States, Europe, and Japan. In the estimation of the U.S.

authorities, both Japan and Western Europe would find it much harder than the United States to deal with a significant increase in oil prices.

As it turned out, this policy backfired. In the same way that Washington decision-makers had underestimated the resolve of the Vietnamese National Liberation Front, they underestimated the chain reaction that their meddling in oil prices would cause within the fledgling OPEC and against the background of the tensions that the Israel-Palestinian conflict had only recently brought to the region. Yet again, however, the United States managed to extract advantages out of a major self-made crisis. To be precise, the United States succeeded in reducing its balance-of-payments deficit. Indeed, by the end of the seventies, it had been eliminated almost entirely. How did the immense hike in oil prices do this?

During the 1970s, while the balance of trade remained deeply in the red, the U.S. balance of payments was improving. However, the situation with the balance of payments was being reversed as a result of a massive strengthening of the U.S. international financial position. In short, the United States managed to attract capital from the rest of the world as the latter sank inexorably into stagflation. As international capital was seeking refuge in the United States, the latter could afford not only to continue with a balance of trade in deficit but, in fact, to allow its trade balance to deteriorate further.

A second silver lining for the United States, following the uncontrollable rise in oil prices in the 1970s, was the massive rise in interest rates spearheaded by spiraling inflation. As central banks struggled to keep the lid on prices, interest rates went through the roof. Setting aside for the moment the worldwide, overwhelming recessionary effects of this development, the rise of interest rates was more effective in destroying the enemies of U.S. foreign policy around the globe than any military operation the United States could ever imagine. Arguably, the chain of events that led to the implosion of Communism in Poland and Yugoslavia began in the 1970s with the sharp rise in interest rates soon after these countries had accepted offers of substantial loans from Western financial institutions. A similar impact occurred in third world countries, where national liberation movements had gained power despite the best efforts of the United States and had borrowed on the international market for the purpose of underwriting much- needed new infrastructure. These economies were to be plunged in a crippling debt crisis following the rise of interest rates from 3 percent to 30 percent in a few short years. In fact, they have never quite recovered since.

As with rising oil prices, so it was with burgeoning interest rates: the U.S. economy (although hit hard by the recession brought on by the rising prices of oil and money) improved its relative financial position, compared not only with Europe and Japan but also with the third world and the Communist nations. By the early 1980s, under the Reagan administration, U.S. policy fully endorsed this new reality and a consensus emerged that the balance of payments ought not to be the focus of attention anymore; that what mattered was the strength of U.S. finance, founded on the strength of its multinationals, particularly in the energy sector, and on the ability to make the dollar accepted internationally (without any form of concrete payment behind it).

In simpler, albeit more emotive, terms, the era that began in the early 1980s is marked by the transformation of the world economy into a periphery from which the United States imports huge quantities of goods with little concern for its balance of payments. Of course, this periphery is not homogeneous. It is, rather, a well-structured realm, complete with two powerful currency zones (the euro zone and Japan–Southeast Asia), which U.S. policy makers alternately bolster or undercut, in response to their assessment of the situation and their evolving overarching objectives.

The United States pays for its deficit to the rest of the world by issuing bonds and treasury bills or by attracting capital through its stock exchanges. Low U.S. inflation is pivotal to this strategy. For unless inflation is kept at close to 1 or 2 percent, the capacity of the U.S. economy to attract capital would be undermined. This is because, if there is relatively high inflation, the asset values and financial assets purchased by incoming capital will decline in value. So from the early 1980s onwards, the main game in Washington was reinforcing U.S. financial capital through the creation of a highly deflationary international environment.

By extension, the rest of the world supplies the United States with commodities at noninflationary prices and, meanwhile, the United States (unlike every other country, including Europe and Japan) does not have to deal with its deficit. This is very similar to the situation that Britain established in relation to India. From the end of the nineteenth century until the Great War, Britain ran a huge balance-of-payments deficit. It managed to maintain it by having India export to the rest of the world and by taxing away, in one way or another, the surplus that India generated through its exports. These capital flows and taxes made it back to the City of London, thus clearing the deficit. This is the model that the United States has been emulating in the last twenty years. Instead, however, of using a single country (as Britain had done), the United States has applied it to the rest of the world.

A brief perusal of the Federal Reserve's research papers over the past ten years shows that the U.S. authorities see the greenback as a strategic asset. The drive to dollarize whole foreign economies, especially in Latin America, is to be understood as part of the same mind set. Dollarization means that the U.S. dollar becomes the country's de facto local currency. The main effect of this move, from the U.S. perspective, is that the demand for dollars then depends not only on the international transactions of other countries but on the domestic transactions of the dollarized economies as well. This gives the United States added political leverage and reduces further the preoccupation with external debt. The reason is simple: as the demand for dollars by foreigners for their own domestic purposes increases, the U.S. balance of payments plays a decreasing role in shaping the dollar's value in the international money markets.

To recapitulate, the Vietnam War put a great deal of strain on the model of world dominance that the United States had been utilizing since 1947. As the cost of waging war in Indochina came to exceed its planned levels by a huge margin, the capacity and willingness of the United States to finance, while controlling, its two creations—the yen and the deutsche mark zones—began to slip. The balance of payments problem intrinsic to this model demanded a new solution, one that involved a redistribution of finance capital away from the yen and deutsche mark zones and back towards the United States. Of course, the shift could not be too sudden since the greenback's two pillars (the Japanese and the European economies) remained, and still are, essential to the United States for their shock-absorbing and effective-demand-enhancing qualities.

Continuing with our review, U.S. officials understood well that the only way the United States could avoid deflation in order to adjust its external balance was by compelling the rest of the world to keep financing the U.S. deficit. Such redistribution of finance capital resembled London's strategy for maintaining a large, long-term balance-of-trade deficit with India. The United States imposed on the rest of the world the role that India played within the British Empire. Tragically, there was a snag. Unlike India, which could export to the rest of the world and thus generate the balance-of-trade surplus which the British would subsequently plunder, the rest of the world cannot export to the rest of the world! It is faced with global excess capacity and a problem of markets.

GEOPOLITICS OF THE NEW DESIGN

The capacity of the United States to pursue its post-Vietnam global design depends on its capacity to maintain a steady flow of capital from the rest of the world. This capacity, in turn, hinges crucially on its political dominance over the rest of the world. Two analysts foreshadowed this when they wrote in 1986, "Even as military assistance and arms sales rocketed upward in the 1970s, many American business figures pressed for an enhanced American capacity for direct intervention abroad."[3]

Anyone who read Bush administration adviser Richard Perle's 1996 report to Israel's then prime minister-elect Netanyahu, "A Clean Break: A New Strategy for Securing the Realm," will immediately recognize the author's emphasis on the nexus between geostrategic concerns and the imperative to secure privileged access to oil.[4] Even if the United States did not need a monopoly over Middle Eastern and Central Asian oil for itself, it would wish to control it in order to guarantee its financial centers a steady flow of petrodollars.

In an ironic sense, the latest war in Iraq might not be about the oil per se. It is about ensuring that whoever controls it buys and sells it in U.S. dollars through the New York commodities exchange. For it is this flow of finance, and to a much lesser extent the ownership of oil, which enables the United States to continue its policy of world dominance through an unbounded balance of payments. Of course, the fact that the oil would be taken over in the post-Saddam era by Bush and his Texan friends does not reduce the administration's enthusiasm.

In November 2000, Richard N. Haass, then director of policy planning in the State Department, strengthened our argument by writing an essay advocating that the United States adopt an "imperial" foreign policy. He defined this as "a foreign policy that attempts to organize the world along certain principles affecting relations between states and conditions within them." This would not be achieved through colonies but through what he termed "informal control," using military might if necessary. Global mechanisms such as international financial markets, the WTO, and the IMF were essential devices for ensuring the dominance of U.S. interests, with the military iron fist backing up the invisible hand of the market.[5]

To give an additional example of the nexus between military dominance and the comparative economic advantage of the United States, it is useful to recount the testimony given to a congressional hearing on Afghanistan in 1998 by John J. Maresca, vice president of oil giant Unocal.[6] In a cheerful prophesy of the 2001 war in Afghanistan, Maresca outlined a rationale for a U.S. invasion of Afghanistan and a future takeover of Central Asia's natural resources. His argument turned on Chinese economic development which, in his view, has to be both abetted and controlled (just as Europe's and Japan's economic development was after the Second World War, we might add).

Maresca implied that, unlike Japan and Europe, China will not willingly liberalize its capital account and, therefore, the flow of capital from China to the United States will be impeded. In simpler words, profits by Chinese, Japanese, European, and, of course, U.S. companies operating in China will not be readily transferable to the United States. Even though Maresca did not spell it out, he was hinting strongly that China's refusal to allow for the free movement of capital to the United States was certain to impede the process of the emerging giant financing the U.S. deficit. The best way to overcome China's recalcitrance, Maresca explained, would be to monopolize the supply of energy in its vicinity. It does not take much genius to see that if China's energy supplies are indeed successfully circumscribed and placed under the control of U.S. companies, it would be easier for the United States, via the WTO and the IMF, to force China's hand and earn concessions permitting China-generated capital to flow to New York.

Moving, for a moment, beyond wars and oil, President Bush's first salvo against global consensus concerned the Kyoto Protocol. The connection between U.S. policies on energy and the environment is evident, but it would be a mistake to think that the Bush administration is merely pursuing the interests of U.S. financial and energy corporations. The anti-green streak of the current administration runs deeper and is related to broader U.S. objectives. In recent years, after stubborn resistance to the idea that the greenhouse effect is real, the administration finally accepted the evident truth: the climate is changing as a result of the greenhouse effect. However, instead of rejoicing, environmentalists were incensed. Why?

The reason is that this acknowledgment was not accompanied by a sense of urgency regarding the need to reverse the effect of global warming. Indeed, the opposite happened. For the last year or so, circles in Washington have been promoting the view that global warming might be bad for most parts of the world but not necessarily bad for the United States. There is, indeed, speculation that U.S. agribusiness will benefit from an increase in global temperatures because, according to estimates based on large-scale computer simulations, the productivity of American agriculture will rise as long as genetically modified seeds are utilized extensively. Meanwhile, with a declining world food production, U.S. "comparative advantage" is predicted to strengthen. Once more, the United States appears to the rest of the world as completely obsessed with the project of remaining unimpeded by its balance-of-trade deficit, even at the planet's expense.

The New Design seems to revolve around the axis of control over energy sources, as well as environmental change, with an explicit view to enhancing the U.S. capacity to draw capital flows from the rest of the world and thus avoid domestic crises due to the growing indebtedness of U.S. families and businesses. If the New Design requires global military campaigns and the alienation of world opinion on matters of global importance (e.g., the environment, world peace), this is deemed a small price to pay for a huge and steady windfall.

POLITICAL REPERCUSSIONS OF THE NEW DESIGN

Many of us wondered why George W. Bush's infantile 2003 State of the Union address sparked a standing ovation, even by Democrats opposed to him. The conventional wisdom is that this is the done thing and American patriotism is a funny creature that allows a Democrat to look at George W. Bush and see not an inane opponent but rather the president of the United States. Be that as it may, this cultural idiosyncrasy cannot extend to the manner in which foes of the Texan oil brigade have kept such an eerie silence. Although the majority of U.S. senators have no direct financial interest in the Great Iraqi Oil Robbery, they all feel quite strongly about preserving the flow of foreign capital through the centers of American finance. Perhaps from their perspective, the Butcher of Baghdad's worst crime was to nominate, back in 1998, the euro as the currency in which Iraqi oil is to be traded!

The fact that the U.S. political establishment, including foes of the Bush administration, seems to fall into line behind the New Design does not mean that the benefits from it are distributed evenly among the American people. If we look closely, there is a rapidly growing division in the U.S. economy between a sector connected to the aeronautic-computer-electronics (ACE) military-industrial complex and the rest of the U.S. economy. Interestingly, although the comparative productivity and competitiveness of the ACE-linked sector is rising vis-à-vis the European and Japanese economies, the rest of the U.S. economy is falling behind. Moreover, the ACE sector is severing its links with the latter, increasing the inequality in jobs, incomes, and opportunities.

Put simply, the latest U.S. economic miracle has nothing to do with the flexibility of its labor markets and the entrepreneurship of the average American; it is a direct product of industries that grew out of its global geostrategic hegemony. Who are the pillars and, at the same time, the beneficiaries of this strategy? One thing we know for sure is that the beneficiaries are not average Americans. In fact, never before have so few Americans had so much while the many had to survive on so little. No, the beneficiaries are three sectors of the U.S. economy: energy multinationals (mostly oil companies), the financial institutions handling the capital flows from the rest of the world, and the ACE industries hooked into the U.S. military. As for the rest of the U.S. domestic economy, and the rest of the world, they are in a state of crisis that will perhaps be permanent.

How have U.S. policy makers managed to maintain political control over this global design? Starting with Japan, we must not forget that the United States re-created a nation with a political apparatus entirely new to it. The loose two-party state imposed by the United States, and effectively written into Japan's constitution, was designed to prevent politicians from having any significant influence on policy. The Japanese bureaucracy is powerful, largely efficient, and autonomous. Thus the people of Japan have become the last Japanese colony, ruled over by a class of bureaucratic entrepreneurs without political ambitions. Though this model provides stability and conformity and is conducive to speedy economic development at times when demand from the United States is high, it is utterly incapable of initiating change, of giving voice to the political aspirations of the Japanese masses, or even of mapping out an autonomous Japanese trade or finance policy.

Examples of Japan's lack of autonomy abound. The United States had ensured that, following the rise of the Southeast Asian tigers, Japan would be selling technological or capital goods to Korea, Malaysia, and Thailand, usually through the transfer of superseded production lines. Interestingly, most regional trade was bilateral (as opposed to trilateral): Southeast Asia was trading directly with the United States and so was Japan. By contrast, the flow of final goods between Southeast Asia and Japan was minuscule. In other words, the United States prevented Japan from establishing an economic zone around it similar to that enjoyed by Germany in the euro zone.

When, following the 1997 crises, Japanese officials realized the benefits lost due to their failure properly to integrate Southeast Asia into the Japanese economy, they tried to make amends. Alas, the United States denied Japan the instruments as well as the opportunities to alter the situation substantially. With the world economy, excluding the United States, in permanent deflation, Japanese factories have no means of making use of their huge capacity, and thus the Japanese economy finds it impossible to transcend a state of perpetual recession.

This makes Japan even more dependent on exporting to the United States. U.S. officials allow Japanese firms access to American consumers but at a hefty price: Japan must forego any plans of becoming a foreign capital importer in competition with the United States. In practical terms, it is forbidden from developing its own international financial policy or from establishing new international bodies for the minimization of financial volatility—especially in Southeast Asia. It is therefore wholly unsurprising that Japanese politicians dare not speak out against U.S. policy at any significant level.

Of the two zones created by U.S. fiat from 1947 to 1955, Europe had a great deal more integrity than Japan. Its industrial capital base was integrated early on—via the Common Agricultural Policy and other European Economic Community (EEC), now European Union (EU), funding mechanisms—with nonindustrial sectors which, though low in productivity, became sources of demand for European industrial goods. Over the period 1947–1995, the United States made (what seemed to be) significant economic sacrifices in order to promote initially the deutsche mark and later economic and monetary union. Whenever the German currency showed signs of weakness the United States bought deutsche marks in solidarity with the Bundesbank. And when the deutsche mark appreciated too much, the United States helped bring it down in solidarity with German industry, even if doing so harmed American companies.

On the political front, the expansionist agenda of the EEC—to engulf Greece, Spain, and Portugal in the early 1980s—was aided and abetted by the United States via NATO. A reasonable observer would surmise that the United States had been more than friendly toward the "European Project." Cynics might add, not without justification, that European unity was indeed an American project—that America thought of European unity and worked diligently toward it long before the Europeans themselves took it to heart. From this viewpoint, the idea that the EU was set up in competition against the United States appears absurd and is best explained as the Europeans' *ex post* rationalization.

Regardless of our degree of cynicism, however, it would take much naïvete to imagine that U.S. ambitions for Europe involved a political union of the type that might spawn an autonomous political program, one that suited Europe independent of global plans for the maintenance of American sovereignty over world finance capital. General de Gaulle understood this well, as he understood that the very constitution of the EEC was not automatically going to engender a European political force. Having also grasped the role of Britain in all this (an economy that the Americans never intended to bond to the deutschmark zone, or the euro zone, but one which they attached directly to the their own dollar zone through the City of London), De Gaulle both exited NATO's military wing and tried, unsuccessfully, to block Britain's entry into the EEC.

More recently, U.S. conduct in Yugoslavia, Chechnya, and now Iraq demonstrates the method by which U.S. policy makers have mixed their support for a European economic sphere of unified trade and capital mobility with support for a weak European political infrastructure.

Remarkably, the U.S. plan, circa 1947, of carving out a European trade zone with a single currency, but no political union, is alive and well. The current U.S. push for extending the EU's borders to the Urals and northern Iraq is highly consistent with this remarkably farsighted plan.

CONCLUSION

European policy makers in Brussels, and their Japanese counterparts in Tokyo, waste countless trees writing and distributing research papers on entrepreneurship and competitiveness, desperately seeking ways of playing catch up with the United States. The most recent such literature from Brussels seems to assume that the U.S. economy is more energetic than those of Europe and Japan because of the superiority of the Protestant ethic, the debilitating effects on incentives caused by overgenerous safety nets, and overly regulated labor markets. The problem with this assumption is that it is at odds with any logically coherent analysis of the global political economy. Europe and Japan always regulated the supply of labor (either institutionally or conventionally) more stringently than the United States. And yet for thirty years the European and Japanese economies (especially Germany) were outstripping that of the United States. Why have things changed?

Conventional wisdom has it that the new economy caused what people in the know refer to as a paradigmatic shift, namely, that capitalism has moved up a gear and Europe's (and Japan's) old ways (with job security and worker's rights) cannot survive in our brave new order. As is so often the case, conventional wisdom's track record at explaining historical shifts is poor. Suppose for a moment that the United States is indeed steaming ahead on the strength of information and computer technologies, fueled by the spirit of American free enterprise and unencumbered by worker-friendly labor laws. If this were so, it should be the case that the U.S. economy is more dynamic, inventive, and innovative across all sectors involving information and computer technologies (compared with their Japanese and European counterparts). But it is not!

The only sectors in which the Americans have overtaken the Europeans and Japanese are those which are intimately linked to the U.S. defense budget—a whopping powerhouse that makes European alleged statism seem like a children's fancy dress party. And yet, Eurocrats and Japanese officials alike make the profound mistake of relying on small picture comparisons which miss the big picture. They observe, for instance, that small firms in the United States have a greater propensity to grow into medium-sized ones. From this they conclude that there must be something about American small business that boosts the U.S. growth rate. Then they look closer but do not find the missing ingredient.

Exhausted, they conclude that the reason must be in the heads of American entrepreneurs; that it must have something to do with the greater fear of remaining uninsured in a rich country where millions have no access to proper medical care. And regrettably, they recommend that perhaps what the Europeans and the Japanese need is a little tough medicine—fewer workers' rights, fewer social benefits, fewer vacations, and, generally, a life more brutal, nasty, and short— in the hope that desperation will stir up waves of entrepreneurship.

What they fail to see is that the United States is not only the land of many small businesses but also the land of the world's largest multinational conglomerates. That U.S. growth in the 1990s was financed by borrowing, so much borrowing from overseas that in the last few years, if all Americans were to sell everything they own, they would still not be able to repay their loans. The question, of course, is why foreigners continue to lend to them, at relatively low interest rates, and without the dollar suffering massive falls. The Panglossian storyline is that foreigners continue to pump money into the U.S. economy because it is so productive. Unfortunately, this is a tautological answer and as such adds nothing to the debate.

Meanwhile, we claim that the real reasons for the renewed U.S. dominance lie elsewhere and have nothing to do with the micro picture. In short, the rest of the world has been placed strategically by U.S. policy makers in a state of permanent deflation. Permanent deflation means high unemployment for the rest of the world regardless of how flexible or inflexible labor markets might be or how entrepreneurial the various peoples are. Europe and Japan have been caught up in the wake of the flow of capital to the United States and are struggling for effective demand. The relatively less-than-dynamic performance of small business sectors across Europe is the effect, rather than the cause, of the relative dominance of the U.S. economy.

There is, we have argued, a great point of difference between the types of dominance that the United States exercised before and after the 1970s so-called oil crises. In the first phase (1947–1979), U.S. efforts to dominate centered upon building up Japan and Europe and fighting regional wars in order to maintain the supply of cheap inputs to the United States and, perhaps more important, to these two zones. The resulting U.S. balance-of-payments deficit boosted these economies further and this, to a large extent, explains why there was no political power in either zone that ever contested American authority (even though some had good cause to quarrel with U.S. administrations, whether for ideological reasons, as in the case of the German Social Democratic Party under Willy Brandt, or for historical ones, as for example, the ultranationalists in the Japanese Liberal Democratic Party).

However, in its second phase the United States adopted a change of design. This New Design required that the rest of the world be in a persistently deflationary state, continually validating U.S. IOUs and, in so doing, protecting the U.S. financial system from a crisis of domestic debt brought about by the unprecedented levels of household and corporate net debt. All of this returns us to the second query with which we opened this paper.

Why have the Germans and the French taken the moral high ground regarding the war on Iraq? Surely it is not because they believe war is wrong or that the United Nations must be consulted. Neither Paris nor Berlin hesitated when it came to bombing Yugoslavia in 1999, or consenting to U.S. invasions in Panama and Grenada or to the brutal terrorism exercised against Nicaragua. The reader will allow us to conclude with an admittedly speculative answer.

Suppose our analysis so far is right in that the latest U.S. economic miracle is financed through capital flows from Europe and the rest of the world. Suppose that Europe has been stagnating for two decades because of the U.S. capacity to impose upon Europeans, by geopolitical means, this type of economic misery. Lastly, suppose that French and German leaders, unlike EU bureaucrats, understand the causes of Europe's malaise. Now, if all these suppositions are true, how should we expect them to interpret the following two announcements of President Bush: first, that he will go to war against an already impoverished people, which will result in U.S. companies gaining exclusive access to the world's second-largest oil fields, and second, that he intends to grant gigantic tax cuts to the richest of his fellow Americans while at the same time boosting government spending (primarily through the defense budget)?

Under the premises above, there is only one possible conclusion that the leaders of "old Europe" must come to: the rest of the world must speed up the rate at which it finances the U.S. deficit (of which continental Europe bears the highest burden). This is tantamount to an acceleration of Europe's deflationary spiral. When these thoughts are combined with the observation that the Bush administration seems uninterested in forging a broad understanding with America's European allies on a wide range of issues (including the Kyoto Protocol, steel tariffs, genetically modified crops, and the International Criminal Court) it is not difficult to see why some European leaders might object. To kill strangers in pursuit of a common objective is one thing, but to consent to such brutality as part of a Grand Design from which one will only lose is quite another.

We believe that the current quarrels between the Bush administration and the Franco-German axis might be a precursor of things to come. Unless the U.S. administration finds some modus vivendi with continental Europe's elites (one that allows the latter to maintain a capacity to reproduce themselves at a sustainable rate), then not only will the U.S. military find itself without allies on the battlefield (except perhaps for some remnants of the British Empire) but also the whole edifice of American global hegemony will totter precariously on the edge of a terrible abyss. We say this because an active U.S. interest in preventing crises of accumulation in Europe and Japan has always underpinned the capacity of these economic zones to continue financing the U.S. deficit. In short, the Bush administration's unilateralism may prove a long- term disaster for U.S. capitalism.

It is now of great historical importance whether U.S. officials will show signs of understanding, as they once did, the importance of supporting capital accumulation in Europe and Asia. Since the Reagan era, no such appreciation has been demonstrated. The real driving force behind U.S. policy has been the voracious appetite of the U.S. economy for foreign capital, a latter day Minotaur single-mindedly concerned with its nourishment. "Old Europe" accepted the role of feeder in the 1980s while the Soviet threat was imminent and in the 1990s, while Clinton was making pleasant noises about inclusive global governance. They now feel that not only is there nothing in it for them but that, in addition, the new Minotaur is too greedy for its own good.

To end on a lighthearted note, one hopes that EU leaders have realized by now how much merriment they must have caused in America's corridors of power when they pronounced three years ago in their Lisbon EU summit that they intended to turn the EU into the world's "most competitive economy by the year 2010." Against the panoply of America's economic, political, and military Global Design, EU leaders were proposing to pit microeconomic reform! U.S. officials must have been shaking in their boots!

8

The Two Wings of the Eagle

WILLIAM K. TABB

Peter Marcuse has written that globalization "is a nonconcept in most usages: a simple catalogue of everything that seems different since, say, 1970, whether advances in information technology, widespread use of air freight, speculation in currencies, increased capital flows across borders, Disneyfication of culture, mass marketing, global warming, genetic engineering, multinational corporate power, new international division of labor, reduced power of nation- states, or post-Fordism."[1] The problem is more than the careless use of words; the inclusion of everything renders the term meaningless. Most important, "the term fogs any effort to separate cause from effect, to analyze what is being done, by whom, to whom, for what and with what effect."[2] To do these things, it is necessary to reframe the discussion. Neither the amorphous globalization discourse of everyday social science nor the previously dominant one of nation- state sovereignty are satisfactory to the task.

Economic thinking is organized around the nation-state, as is that of political science. The sovereignty of nations is assumed, and the task is how to ensure greater cooperation in solving mutual problems. The world has been conceptualized as a system of sovereign states and we speak, for example, of *international* trade. It is now suggested that as a result of an altogether amorphous globalization process, the symmetry between states and markets has broken down. Some assert that the nation was the proper unit of analysis for only a short historical period, perhaps from the late-nineteenth to the late-twentieth century. Others conclude that because relationships are increasingly networked, they are not hierarchical or territorial. In this view, since individuals and organizations are enmeshed in worldwide webs and exhibit multiple and competing loyalties, the territorial period is over.

In our view, the focus on territorial integrity has always been misleading for most of the peoples of the world. Through much of history there have been empires, by which we mean a system of interaction in which a dominant metropole exerts effective political sovereignty over the internal and external policy of the subordinate periphery.

The intermediate term between an entirely amorphous *globalization* and the more concrete *empire* is *hegemony* and, like empire, hegemony is used in many ways. In mainstream international relations studies it is widely accepted that in the post–Second World War period the United States built what has been called "stakeholder" hegemony. It is argued that by making institutions of international policy-making more accountable and transparent, adhering to the rule of law, and vetting policies with allies, the United States made an ongoing but unequal partnership acceptable to other countries. Allies who cooperate with Washington have influence on the ways in which its power is exercised. This institutional bargain reduces the penchant of the hegemon for unilateralism by binding the hyperpower to a set of rules which it has itself been crucial in creating. It is worthwhile for others to submit to American leadership, in this framework, because American power is constrained. And the United States, by acting with restraint and in a reliable manner, gains wider cooperation. It is this accommodation which is widely said to be threatened by the Bush administration's turn toward unilateralism.

What is actually at issue here is the choice between two U.S. imperial strategies: a hegemony geared primarily to promoting neoliberal globalization on terms particularly favorable to the United States, and an alternative hegemony that steers toward the establishment of a more formal U.S. empire. These two paths represent alternative strategies that an imperial ruling class may choose between, but in many respects they may also be complementary.

The concern on the part of liberal institutionalists with the new unilateral vehemence in U.S. economic and foreign policy comes from their analysis of the value of the postwar stakeholder hegemony model. They argue that by facilitating a more open and liberal world economy, American primacy fostered global prosperity. They say that economic interdependence creates peaceful relations between states. This Clintonian position is summed up with the tag that no two countries which have a McDonald's have ever gone to war. Reagan's invasion of McDonald's-rich Panama neatly reveals the liberals' unspoken assumptions. U.S. military intervention in Latin America is, by definition, not war.

The Bush Doctrine, on the other hand, is seen by its proponents as one in which the United States, by creating "peace and democracy" through preemptive war and regime change, creates conditions for economic development. Investors are more likely to send cash to places with stable democratic governments respectful of property rights. In this framing it is the active use of the hegemonic capacities of the United States that is conducive to expanding world trade and investment. The threat and use of force become policies for increasing the economic well- being of the poor and oppressed. Such assertiveness can contribute much more than the paltry and often ineffectual policies of, say, the World Bank. Of course it is rarely put quite this boldly, but increasingly the argument is being made. More straightforward commentators strike a note of self-satisfaction and self-interest, declaring that "empire rewards those who run them with goods, honor, and celebrity status. And for all the disclaimers about the white man's burden or its contemporary equivalent, few of us who get the chance to share these rewards disdain them."[3] The U.S. elite shall do well by doing good.

Shaping and expanding the "zone of democracy" through the use of military power dominates the Bush II presidency. Being seen as a member of "coalitions of the willing" is the key to economic aid and better treatment in trade negotiations. It has always been true that staying on the good side of the powerful is important. Nonetheless, it appears to many that some line has been crossed—perhaps from hegemony to outright empire. Hegemony refers to a situation in which one state is powerful enough to maintain the essential rules governing interstate relations and is willing to do so. An empire is a form of domination in which one state seizes power and rules over others. Empire subjects peoples to unequal rule. One nation's government determines who rules another society's political and economic life. If such a definition is accepted, then it is reasonable to speak of the American Empire, even if it is an empire different from those of Britain and Rome.

In fact, the two perspectives overlap. Liberal institutionalists and even some self-styled leftists advocate the reluctant acceptance of responsibility for peoples and lands that must be rescued from the primitive "Balkan" violence that threatens to engulf them if left on their own. This human rights rationale for intervention is attractive to many liberals for whom discussion of oil and empire is distasteful. For the more honest within this camp the disagreement is tactical and focuses on whether an empire relying only on force and functioning without international approval can succeed.

To radicals, such an understanding is fundamentally flawed. Imperialism is now, as it always has been, a conscious class project of the dominant sectors of the advanced economies using their states' ability to project force to gain or retain control over important resources and to maintain a world order in which their interests come before all others. This does not mean that it doesn't help if purveyors of imperialism speak in idealist terms. The imperialists claim to be disseminating law and order and to be promoting justice, education, peace, and prosperity. This is as true today as it was a century ago at the height of the "white-man's-burden" interventions, invasions, and regime changes. Deception and perhaps self-deception make the project easier, but it must be condemned and resisted no matter how it is packaged.

A number of commentators have noted that U.S. diplomacy has had two languages: "one line descending from the macho axioms of Theodore Roosevelt, the other from the presbyterian cant of Woodrow Wilson."[4] It is of course no accident that the first Roosevelt is Bush's favorite president. The liberals who invoke human rights are more in the rhetorical frame of Woodrow Wilson's Fourteen Points, but neither Bush nor any other U.S. leader has hesitated to draw some from column A and some from column B or to speak of the U.S. primacy as if it does God's work in the world.

We may want to think of the two wings of the eagle. One, the Wilsonian, is multilateralist and concerned with constructing global state governance institutions. The other is the unilateralist shock-and-awe approach, which holds that the way to gain respect is to use a big stick. The first tends to be liberal in the terms of U.S. politics and to represent transnational capital and international finance, both of which prefer an open trading system based on the stakeholder hegemony discussed earlier. The second comes from the cowboy capitalism side— the oil industry, the military contractors, and the religious crusaders. The first might have been better represented by a Gore presidency; the latter is happy with a Bush White House. No matter who is in the Oval Office, both wings have their needs met even if the strategic vision is somewhat different. In terms of the exercise of state power, any attempt at a firm differentiation of the military, economic, and political would ride roughshod over their interdependence and interaction. Nonetheless, the embrace of a religious crusade to remake the world and to force a craven "Old Europe" into a more disciplined understanding of its true place differs from what we could have expected from an Al Gore. These are mainly differences of strategy and posture with which to achieve the agreed upon goal of U.S. dominance and control over other people's resources, labor power, and markets. Whether a guiding multilateral leadership or an assertive unilateralism is the best way to achieve these goals is a dispute within a common class outlook. This is not to say, however, that such differences do not have important consequences—indeed, one strategy or the other may prove more efficacious at a particular point in time.

What we have today is a return to aspirations of old-style imperial domination and a claim to authority over others and to solo decision-making privileges that is breathtaking. When Bush said on September 20, 2001, to a joint session of Congress, that "our war on terror begins with Al Qaeda but does not end there. It will not end until every terrorist group of global reach has been found, stopped and defeated," he was announcing a permanent war footing for an indefinite length of time—this was to be the single-minded focus of his presidency. The warning to the rest of the world was famously made clear in his statement: "Every nation in every region now has a decision to make. Either you are with us or you are with the terrorists." Vice President Cheney said the United States may have to take military action against "forty to fifty countries" and that the war could last half a century or more.

Whether the American Empire is a matter of enlightened self-interest under which free markets and democracy shall flourish, or whether we are seeing a frank avowal of the policies of state power unwilling to be constrained by respect for other countries unless forced to do so, we have a situation which makes many in the world unhappy. It has been remarked that "one reads about the world's desire for American leadership only in the United States [but] everywhere else one reads about American arrogance and unilateralism."[5]

Primacy brings greater freedom of action over a range of activities and earns cooperation on terms favorable to the hegemon. There is nothing uniquely bad about the United States' quest for primacy, nor is there any uniqueness of national character in the sense that any other major capitalist state formation having such opportunity would not act in a similar manner. The debate among the elite is a different one: What is the best manner in which the United States should wield its power? It is a given that "the USA is Number One" and that the U.S. elite, for understandable reasons, prefer having more power rather than less, and they plan to keep it that way. This naturally means that a willful United States can impose devastating costs on any who would cross it. The debate among the elite is tactical: Should the United States, able to act unilaterally, do so? Does it serve U.S. interests to be or appear to be insensitive to others' concerns? That is, does the United States benefit from the naked show of force and harsh employment of its military capacities, or does the United States do better acting with others multilaterally and through global governance institutions like the United Nations and the World Trade Organization? The shift under the post–September 11 George W. Bush has been a sharp one. In 2000, in his second presidential debate, he said that the world would be attracted to an America that was strong but humble and would be repulsed if the nation used its power in an arrogant fashion. As his liberal critics now say, his position then was correct.

But for those further to the left there is a different question: Should the United States run the world? This is not a debate over strategy, unilateralism, or multilateralism. It is a question of how we create a world in which all people's lives, hopes, prospects are equally valued, and how we can live together in mutual respect so as to replace war and exploitation as the governing mechanisms of the world system.

Those who would raise this set of issues need to realize that the current turn of George W. Bush is based on the same Washington Consensus ideology that marked the Clinton regime. "The terrorists attacked the World Trade Center, and we will defeat them by expanding and encouraging world trade," was Bush's position shortly after September 11, 2001, "seeming to imply," as the *New York Times* commented, "that trade somehow was among the concerns of the terrorists who brought down the towers." Robert Zoellick, the U.S. trade representative opined that opponents of corporate-led globalization might have "intellectual connections" with the terrorists. The president declared: "Open trade is not just an economic opportunity, it is a moral imperative. Trade creates jobs for the unemployed. When we negotiate for open markets, we're providing new hope for the world's poor. And when we promote open free trade, we are promoting political freedom."

Such thinking found its way into the September 2002 *National Security Strategy of the United States of America* submitted by the White House to the Congress. This document laid out the new preemptive doctrine and promised to maintain military supremacy over all potential rivals indefinitely. But it also tied the Washington Consensus tightly to this Bush Doctrine: "We will actively work to bring the hope of democracy, development, free markets, and free trade to every corner of the world." It lists among its policies lower marginal tax rates and pro-growth legal and regulatory policies which every nation should adopt because "the concept of 'free trade' arose as a moral principle even before it became a pillar of economics. If you can make something that others value, you should be able to sell it to them. If others make something that you value, you should be able to buy it. That is real freedom, the freedom for a person—or a nation—to make a living." To any honest observer this is not an ideology of freedom or democracy. It is a system of control, an economics of empire.

The problems of underdevelopment are likely to get worse in most less-developed countries in coming decades, in some cases considerably worse. It is problematic whether the Bush gamble at transforming the region through its sponsorship of regime change will make this situation better. In the world today hundreds of millions of people are starving, hundreds of millions of adults are illiterate, and hundreds of millions of children do not attend school. Billions of people have no access to basic sanitation or low-cost medicines. Epidemic disease has returned on a scale unimaginable in the 1960s. Whether under these conditions the further militarization of the world makes sense over an alternative agenda of serious development that would cost far less in money terms, to say nothing of lives, needs to be considered by Americans. That is, if we can get them to turn off television news and think about these issues in terms of solidarity with other members of the global human community.

A left alternative, unsurprisingly, would require policies which are the exact opposite of the Washington Consensus model. That model favors trade liberalization and export-led growth, financial market liberalization and uncontrolled capital movements, privatization and less social provision of goods and services, lower taxes, fiscal- and monetary-policy austerity, and what is called labor market deregulation and labor market flexibility. When we criticize the policies that the global state economic governance institutions have imposed, we must not forget that these policies were imposed globally under the rule of the Wilsonian wing of the U.S. ruling class. These policies increase economic insecurity and a sense of powerlessness, which is only accentuated by the Bush administration's national chauvinism and use of overwhelming violence. To reverse these developments will take a broad-based coalition of the morally concerned who want this country to be about very different values. But to achieve another world that we believe is possible and necessary requires a deeper critique, class analysis, and the self- organization of a class-conscious movement for radical transformation. Our critique must be of both the Teddy Roosevelt and the Wilson (or Bush and Clinton) wings of this bird of prey; it must be an anti-imperialist critique.

PART THREE

Resistance

The history of capitalism is replete with examples of struggles against imperialism. The most significant of these have for obvious reasons taken place in the poor countries of the third world. This has led to a number of historic defeats for imperialism—for example, in Cuba, Vietnam, and Iran. These resistance struggles have taken different political forms but nonetheless all exhibit the desire of people everywhere for self-determination, independent of foreign powers.

At the center of world capitalism support for imperialism has often been widespread, even among the leaders of workers and oppositional political parties. However, when presented with strong resistance in the periphery exposing the true character of imperialism, popular resistance often emerges in the center as well. A broad and militant antiwar movement in the United States helped to force the end of the U.S. war against the Vietnamese people. Today, an even larger antiwar movement, worldwide in scope, grew rapidly in the run-up to the U.S. invasion and occupation of Iraq. This movement declined once the war began but will likely resurface as the situation in Iraq more and more takes on the character of a war of liberation by the Iraqi people.

Before the invasion and occupation of Iraq, a worldwide global justice movement was built and was showing signs of becoming increasingly anti-imperialist. The events of September 11, 2001, created grave difficulties for this movement, as the U.S. government used the "war on terrorism" to eliminate civil liberties and curtain dissent. Nevertheless, the global justice movement is still very much alive, and should it and the antiwar movement come to be fully supported by labor movements, the struggle against imperialism could enter a decisive new phase.

9

Confronting the Empire

SAMIR AMIN

From the 1980s on, and with increased momentum after the collapse of the Soviet system, the ruling class in the United States, whether Democrat or Republican, began drawing up a hegemonic program. Carried away by its military power, and without any competitor able to temper its fantasies, the United States chose to reinforce its domination by deploying a military strategy aiming at planetary control. An early series of interventions—in the Gulf, Yugoslavia, Central Asia, Palestine, and Iraq—introduced this strategy for endless wars to be "made in the USA," planned and decided unilaterally by Washington.

The political strategy that accompanied this program defined the pretexts for it, whether these had to do with terrorism, the fight against drug trafficking, or with accusations of producing weapons of mass destruction.

Accusations of producing dangerous weapons—made today against Iraq and North Korea, but tomorrow against any convenient state—pale beside the actual use of these weapons by the United States. The United States used nuclear weapons at Hiroshima and Nagasaki and chemical weapons in Vietnam, and it is threatening the further use of nuclear weapons in future conflicts. Such pretexts are only propaganda tools, in the sense that Goebbels gave that term: they are useful perhaps to manipulate U.S. opinion but less and less credible elsewhere.

The idea of "preventive war," now claimed as a "right" by Washington, does away with any notion of international law. The United Nations Charter forbids recourse to war except in cases of legitimate self-defense, and it allows military intervention only under strict conditions, any response having to be measured and provisional. All specialists in international law know that the wars undertaken since 1990 have been illegitimate, and that those who bear the responsibility for them are therefore war criminals. Indeed, the United States, with the cooperation of other countries, is already treating the United Nations as the fascist states treated the League of Nations.

The abolition of the common rights of all peoples is already underway. The principle of the equality of all peoples has been replaced by the distinction between a "master race" (*Herrenvolk*)—the people of the United States—and other peoples. The existence of those peoples that do not belong to the U.S. master race can only be tolerated if they do not constitute a threat to the ambitions of those who consider themselves the masters of the planet. This master race reserves the right to conquer whatever living space it judges necessary for itself and for those peoples it supports.

What are the national interests that the U.S. ruling class considers as the basis for this right?

This is a class that recognizes only one objective—that of making money. The North American state is openly at the service of satisfying the demands of the dominant segment of capital made up of U.S. multinationals.

We, therefore, have all become "redskins," the contemptuous name reserved for the Native Americans, in the eyes of the Washington establishment—that is to say, peoples who have the right to exist only in so far as they do not frustrate the expansion of U.S.-based multinational capital. We have been promised that resistance to the United States will be crushed using any and every means, even extermination if necessary. If it is a question of making an additional $15 million in profit for the American multinationals at the expense of 300 million victims, there will be no hesitation. The "rogue state" par excellence, to borrow the language used by presidents Bush Senior and Junior, as well as by Clinton, is none other than the United States itself.

The U.S. program is certainly imperialist in the most brutal sense of that word, but it is not "imperial" in the sense that Antonio Negri has given the term, since it does not aim to manage the societies of the planet in order better to integrate them into a coherent capitalist system. Instead, it aims only to loot their resources. All this is part and parcel of the reduction of social thought to the mantras of vulgar economics, the single-minded focus on maximizing the financial profitability of dominant capital in the short term, putting the military at the disposal of this capital, and delinking this capital from any system of human values. Such capital is behind the barbaric expansionism capitalism carries within itself, substituting a demand of absolute submission to the so-called laws of the market for human values.

Throughout its history, U.S. capitalism has shown itself to be more willing than European varieties to take such steps. Politically, the U.S. state is designed to serve the economy and nothing else, abolishing the contradictory and dialectical relationship between economy and politics. The genocide carried out against the Native Americans, the enslavement of the blacks, the manipulation of ethnic and racial conflict by the ruling class (at the expense of the maturation of class consciousness) have all combined to produce the political monopoly of U.S. society by the single party of capital. Both segments of this party share the same strategic global vision, though they address their rhetoric to different "constituencies," themselves drawn from the less than half of U.S. society that believes sufficiently in the system to bother voting.

Not benefitting from the tradition by which the social democratic worker's parties and the Communists marked the formation of modern European political culture, American society does not have the ideological instruments at its disposal to allow it to resist the dictatorship of capital. On the contrary, capital shapes every aspect of this society's way of thinking and reproduces itself by reinforcing the kind of deep-seated racism that allows U.S. society to see itself as constituting a master race. Playboy Clinton, Cowboy Bush: this slogan from India rightly emphasizes the nature of the single party that manages the so-called U.S. democracy.

For this reason, the U.S. program is not the simple attempt to attain hegemony familiar from ancient and modern history, involving a vision of problems having coherent answers, whether based on economic exploitation or political inequality. Instead, it is infinitely more brutal in its simple and extreme unilateral conception, and it is close to the Nazi program, which was also based on the principle of a master race. The U.S. program has nothing whatsoever to do with the beliefs of certain American liberal academics, who see U.S. hegemony as "benign."

If it should continue, this program can only lead to growing chaos, which will continually call for increasingly brutal management, with no strategic long-term vision. Finally, Washington will not even attempt to support its real allies, something which always requires knowing how to make concessions. Fake governments, like that of Karzai in Afghanistan, will manage things better as long as military power supports a belief in the "invincibility" of the United States. Hitler did not think any differently.

An examination of the connections between the criminal U.S. program and the realities of dominant capitalism made up of the countries of the Triad (the United States, Europe, and Japan) will allow us to understand its strengths and weaknesses.

General opinion, as promoted by the unreflective media, has it that U.S. military power only constitutes the tip of the iceberg, and that it represents the extension of American superiority in all areas, notably economic, but even political and cultural. For this reason, it is widely believed that submission to the hegemony that America pretends to is inevitable.

However, an examination of economic realities undermines this view. The U.S. production system is far from being the most efficient in the world. On the contrary, almost none of its sectors would be certain of beating competitors in the truly free market dreamed of by liberal economists. The U.S. trade deficit, which increases year by year, went from $100 billion in 1989 to $450 billion in 2000. Moreover, this deficit involved practically all areas of production—even the surplus once enjoyed by the United States in the area of high-technology goods, which stood at $35 billion in 1990, has now turned into a deficit.

Competition between Ariane rockets and those of NASA, as well as between Airbus and Boeing, testifies to American vulnerability. U.S. producers must compete against high- technology products from Europe and Japan, manufactured goods from China, Korea, and other Asian and Latin American industrialized countries, as well as agricultural produce from Europe and the southern cone of Latin America. The United States probably would not be able to win were it not for the recourse to extra-economic means, a clear violation of the principles of liberalism the United States imposes on its competitors.

In fact, the United States enjoys comparative advantages only in the armaments sector, precisely because this sector largely operates outside the rules of the market and benefits from state support. This may bring some benefits to the civil sphere, the Internet being the best-known example, but it also causes serious distortions that handicap many sectors of production. The U.S. economy lives parasitically to the detriment of its partners in the world system: "The United States depends for 10 per cent of its industrial consumption on goods whose import costs are not covered by the exports of its own products,"[1]

The economic growth of the Clinton years, vaunted as the result of a "liberalism" that Europe was unfortunately resisting, was in fact largely chimerical, and was, in any case, not generalizable because it depended on capital transfers that caused the stagnation of partner economies. For all sectors of the real production system, U.S. growth during this period was not better than that of Europe. The "American miracle" was fed exclusively by a growth in expenditure produced by growing social inequalities (for example, in financial and personal services and the legions of lawyers and private police forces). In this sense, Clinton's liberalism prepared the conditions for the reactionary wave and the victory of Bush Junior. Moreover, as Emmanuel Todd writes, "Blown up by fraud, American GNP begins to resemble, in terms of statistical accuracy, that of the Soviet Union."[2]

The world produces, and the United States, which has practically no funds in reserve, consumes. The U.S. advantage is that of a predator whose deficit is covered by loans from others. The means put in place by Washington to compensate for deficiencies are of various kinds, including repeated unilateral violations of liberal principles; arms exports (60 percent of the world market) largely imposed on subaltern allies, such as the Persian Gulf countries that never use these weapons; and the search for greater profits from oil, which presupposes greater control over the producers—the real reason for the wars in Central Asia and Iraq.

A large, indeed indispensable, part of the U.S. deficit is covered by contributions of capital from Europe, Japan, and the South—from oil-rich countries and comprador classes in every country of the third world, the poorest included. To this are added the additional sums brought in from servicing the debt that has been forced on practically all the countries on the periphery of the world system. The reasons behind the continuing capital movements that feed the parasitism of the U.S. economy and society, and that allow this superpower to live from day to day, are certainly complex. But they have nothing to do with the supposed laws of the market that are at once rational and unchangeable.

The solidarity between the dominant segments of transnational capital and the members of the Triad is real, and it explains their rallying to globalized neoliberalism. The United States is seen as the defender, militarily if necessary, of common interests, though Washington hardly intends to share fairly the profits of its leadership. On the contrary, it seeks to make its allies into vassals and is only ready to make minor concessions to its junior allies in the Triad. Will this conflict of interests within dominant capital lead to the breakup of the Atlantic alliance? This is unlikely, but not impossible.

The real conflict is situated on a different terrain, that of political culture. In Europe, a left alternative that would force a break with neoliberalism is still possible. However, this would require abandoning the vain hope that the United States will submit to the same neoliberal discipline it enforces on others, competing with European capital on a level playing field and permitting Europe an independent foreign policy. The capital surplus that Europe has until now been happy to place in the United States could be used to launch a European economic and social renewal, which would be impossible without this capital surplus. Were Europe to give priority to its own economic and social growth in this way, the artificial health of the U.S. economy would collapse, and the American ruling class would be confronted by its own social problems. That is what I mean by saying that Europe will either be on the left or it will not be at all.

To get there, however, we must dispense with the illusion that the liberal game should, or could, be played honestly by all and then things would get better. The United States cannot give up the asymmetric practice of liberalism, since this is the only way that it can compensate for its deficiencies. U.S. prosperity comes at the price of others' stagnation.

Why, therefore, do capital flows that benefit the United States continue? Probably because for many the United States is a country for the rich and the safest refuge for them—this is the case for investments made by the comprador bourgeoisie of the third world. But what explains European attitudes? The "liberal virus," together with a naïve belief that the United States will end up accepting market rules, has a certain power over public opinion. The principle of the free circulation of capital, made sacred by the IMF, enables the United States to cover its deficit by pumping in financial surpluses generated elsewhere as a result of neoliberal policies, while submitting only very selectively to neoliberal discipline. However, for dominant capital the advantages of the system overcome its inconveniences—this is the price that it must pay to Washington in order to ensure the permanence of the system.

Countries described as "indebted poor countries" are forced to pay, but there is one indebted powerful country that will never pay its debts. The militarist program chosen by the U.S. establishment should be seen in this perspective, being nothing other than an admission that the United States has no other means at its disposal to impose its economic hegemony.

The causes of the weakening of the U.S. production system are complex. They are certainly not conjunctural, and they cannot be corrected by the adoption of a correct rate of exchange, for example, or by putting in place a more favorable balance between salaries and productivity. On the contrary, they are structural. The poor quality of general education and training in the United States—the product of a deep-rooted prejudice in favor of the private to the detriment of the public sector—is one of the main reasons for the profound crisis of U.S. society.

One should, therefore, be surprised that the Europeans, far from drawing the logical conclusions from observing the deficiencies of the U.S. economy, are actively going about imitating it. Here, too, the liberal virus does not explain everything, even if it fulfills some useful functions for the system in paralyzing the left. Widespread privatization and the dismantling of public services will only reduce the comparative advantages from which "Old Europe" still benefits. However, whatever damage these measures will cause in the long term, they offer dominant capital, which lives in the short term, the chance of making additional profits.

The militarist program adopted by the United States now threatens all peoples. It is the expression of the logic adopted by Hitler—to change social and economic relations by military force in favor of the master race of the day. This program, now filling the foreground, overdetermines all political circumstances, since the pursuit of such a program weakens advances obtainable through social and democratic struggle. Halting the U.S. militarist program becomes, therefore, a major aim and responsibility for all.

Success in this struggle will depend on the capacity of people everywhere to rid themselves of liberal illusions, since there will never be an authentically liberal globalized economy. This is the case despite all the means used to make us believe otherwise. The World Bank operates as a sort of ministry of propaganda for Washington extolling democracy, good governance, or the reduction of poverty—it has no other function. Joseph Stiglitz, made the subject of considerable media buzz for rediscovering some elementary truths and asserting them with an air of authority, has nevertheless been unable to call into question the prejudices of vulgar economics.

The reconstruction of a Southern Front capable of giving the peoples of Asia, Africa, and Latin America together in solidarity across three continents the capacity to make their voices heard, will require liberating ourselves from the illusion that a globalized liberal system without assymetry would help the peoples of the third world. Is it not ridiculous to watch the countries of the South insist upon "putting liberal principles into practice without discrimination," thus gaining the applause of the World Bank? When was the World Bank ever concerned with defending the third world against the United States?

The struggle against U.S. imperialism and the U.S. militarist program is a struggle shared by all peoples, from its major victims in Asia, Africa, and Latin America, to the peoples of Europe and Japan, who are condemned to subordinate positions, and also to the people of the United States themselves. We should salute the courage of all those at the heart of the beast who have refused to submit, as their predecessors refused to submit to the McCarthyism of the 1950s. Like those who dared to resist Hitler, they have merited all the praise that history can heap upon them.

Will the dominant class in the United States be able to carry forward the criminal program behind which it has rallied? This is not an easy question to answer—little or nothing in the history of U.S. society prepares it for the task. The single party of capital, whose power in the United States is not contested, has thus far not given up on military adventure, and therefore the responsibility of this class as a whole cannot be downplayed. The power of Bush Junior is not that of a clique of armament and oil producers. As has been the case in the entire modern history of the United States, the dominant power comprises a coalition of the sectoral interests of capital, falsely described as "lobbies."

However, this coalition can only govern if other segments of capital accept it. Clearly, political, diplomatic, and even military setbacks could encourage the minority in the U.S. establishment who are ready to renounce the military adventures the country is engaged in. To hope for more than this seems to me to be as naïve as to have hoped, at the height of the Nazi regime, that the assassination attempts against Hitler would succeed.

If the Europeans had reacted in 1935 or 1937, they could have stopped the Hitler regime. The failure to react until September 1939 cost the lives of tens of millions. Let us act together in the hope that a response to the present Washington neo-Nazis will come sooner.[3]

10

The Parameters of Resistance

AMIYA KUMAR BAGCHI

As imperialism spirals out of control, and as the manifestations of its wickedness penetrate every pore of human existence everywhere, the resistance against it also has emerged from every cell of social and political organization, taking many diverse forms that defy easy encapsulation. As the forms of protest and resistance have multiplied, the problem of choosing an appropriate political strategy has become that much more difficult. Is the resistance to be mounted only globally? Are we to fight only licentious finance and the greed of marauding transnational corporations and leave everything else to be settled after that global fight is won? Or are we to fight every little tyranny everywhere—the corruption of municipal officials, the arrogance of party bosses seeking to control local democracy, the callousness of public hospital authorities? And are we to treat as enemies every political formation that provides succor and comfort to such petty tyrants and overweening bureaucrats?[1]

In much of the third world, including the subcontinent of South Asia, a line seems to divide the antisystemic or anti-imperialist struggles into two groups. On the one hand, there are those who believe in the necessity of squaring up for battle against global transnational capital and fighting to reverse the policies that have allowed it to subvert and control all major governments. The adherents of this view think that long-term strategies for capturing state power have to be pursued toward that end. On the other hand, others are convinced that the fight against tyrannies that are crippling the lives of people has to be conducted here and now.

In fact, the *political activists*, if that is a name we can give to the first group, have to deal with local issues—and they have to prove their sincerity and competence in dealing with them. Such constructive engagements are necessary, in addition to their ideology, for them to build their base of support and strengthen popular resistance against the oppression of capital and the state apparatus. There are also some among the *moral resisters*, to give a name to the other group, who are not averse to seeking the help of the state apparatus to right the wrongs they are fighting against. But there are some moral resisters who think that the state, as such, is an evil institution and its embrace is to be avoided at all cost.

This division, however blurred at the edges, between the political activists and the moral resisters has often made it difficult for resistance movements to unify in the past. The division has generally been described as one between those movements whose ideologies focus on the control of state power and those that seek to remedy evils without bothering about who controls the state. By and large, so-called neutral academics have approved of the moral resisters rather than those they see as seeking power. The division has also been described as a divide between the communist or socialist view of resistance movements and the Foucauldian view, with its focus on the cellular nature of oppressive structures and their inevitable appearance under any state, however benignly it may try to operate.

I have never been able to accept this dichotomy as a valid representation of today's resistance to imperialist capitalism, that is, the actual capitalism of the twentieth and twenty-first centuries. The fight against imperialism must encompass all aspects of life, including the forms of ideology, the state apparatus, and the so-called civil society as well. The fight has to be fought by uniting all genuine anti-imperialist formations. The immense diversity of human existence, and the many different ways oppression burdens that existence, must be part of our understanding of why different forms of resistance arise in different contexts.

Divisions among the anti-imperialist forces, caused partly by the lack of such an appreciation, have helped sustain and expand imperialism throughout its history. The greatest damage to the international socialist movement in the twentieth century was caused by the Sino- Soviet rift of 1960. One major cause of the rift was the failure of the Soviet leadership to appreciate that socialism might develop along different paths in different historical settings. The congealing of the dictatorship of the proletariat into the dictatorship of the party bureaucracy also made the actually existing socialism impervious to the specific demands of peoples with different histories and different trajectories. The fight with capitalist-imperialist forces exhausted the Soviet regime and gave a handle to the imperialist forces to incite nationalities and ethnic groups against the groups supported by the Soviet bloc. This history has left many genuine antisystemic movements suspicious of all formations that support any party holding power in however subordinate a fashion.

On the other hand, the overwhelming nature of the onslaught of imperialism in its latest incarnation has convinced many in the social movements that it is not enough to fight local tyrannies and local oppression. Instead, it is necessary to seek allies who are prepared to fight the system in all its ramifications, attacking the taproot of imperialism. The ecological movement in India, for example, which began as a protest against the indiscriminate felling of trees by timber merchants, endangering the livelihood and water resources of the people and women in particular, was then taken up by all left-oriented groups resisting the environmental devastation by profit-hunting capital. The ecological movements were present in strength in the recent Asian Social Forum held in Hyderabad, India.

One of the unfortunate legacies of the actually existing socialism, and the political parties associated with it, was a fascination with big factories, big dams, and big projects in general. They symbolized for them, and for many noncommunist nationalists, the drive of all oppressed people toward industrialization and their search for freedom from degrading poverty. Jawaharlal Nehru, the first prime minister of independent India, who shared some of the values of the global socialist movement, famously called these dams and factories the temples of modern India. However, many of the factories and dams were located in sites that had provided shelter and livelihood to the peasants and forest-users of interior India; those people were displaced and derived few benefits from the projects that destroyed their homes. Various groups gave voice to the discontent and desperation of the displaced, but there was a tendency among organized communist movements to look upon these protests with suspicion. However, when the Silent Valley in Kerala, one of the richest habitats of subtropical flora and fauna in the world, was threatened by a hydroelectric power project, the movement to protect it was spearheaded by the Kerala Sahitya Shastra Parishad, a body organized chiefly by communist activists to spread literacy and raise the awareness of science and health care among ordinary people. Because of the protests, the project was dropped and the Silent Valley was saved.

The construction of a dam across the Narmada River in western India brought the movement against big dams to a head, attracting global attention. The opposition movement was known as Narmada Bachao Andolan (Save the Narmada). Despite a protest movement lasting over a decade, a big dam was constructed across the Narmada. It has already displaced thousands of Adivasis (indigenous peoples) and non-Adivasi peasants in the catchment area of the river. The project is economically unsound, and it may fail to achieve its original political rationale, to deliver water to the rich farmers in Gujarat. The main leaders of the protest movement, Medha Patekar and Baba Amte, have built around it the National Alliance for People's Movements (NAPM). There was mutual suspicion between the NAPM and the organized left parties in the beginning, but fortunately, in the face of the common enemy of unbridled globalization by the rich, of the rich, and for the rich, they are now fighting shoulder to shoulder against the WTO and the structural adjustment and privatization programs of the central government in India.

Similar movements opposed the privatization of the Bharat Aluminium Company (BALCO), which is located on Adivasi land in today's Chhattisgarh in central India. That land was taken over by the government on the explicit understanding that it would be used only for public purposes. The sale of the company to a blacklisted private enterprise at an absurdly low price and the endangerment of the workers' jobs led to a joint protest by the Adivasi residents and the workers of the affected company. The protesters took their grievance to the Supreme Court. The court treated the valuation of BALCO by the government-appointed firm as valid and dismissed the case. Class-biased judgments are as common in India as in the United States, after all. Again, the ubiquitous influence of capitalist values was demonstrated. However, neither the Narmada Bachao Andolan nor the protest against the privatization of BALCO disappeared from people's memory and they continue to figure regularly in the repertoirc of ecological movements and the movements orchestrated by left parties. The Foucauldian movements and the Marxist political parties can come together after all.

South Asia, along with west Asia, and several countries of East and Southeast Asia, remain bastions of male chauvinism. A principal marker of religious and ethnic fundamentalisms is their tendency to revere women as icons while oppressing them as human beings. One of the most hopeful signs of the unfolding of people's consciousness of their rights as human beings in South Asia during the closing decades of the twentieth century has been the growth of the women's movement against gender, class, and state oppression and exploitation based on women's seclusion at home. The women's movement has been active in demanding stringent measures against domestic violence, the enormous incidence of female feticide carried out with the help of modern reproductive technology, and the murder of women for dowry and in the pursuit of more lucrative wives. Women have also protested against the use of many birth control technologies that endanger their health but are profitable for transnational companies and the aid agencies colluding with them. The movement has demanded the reservation of positions for women in local governments, in state assemblies, and in the central parliament.

In Gujarat, perhaps the most developed capitalist state in India, beginning in February 2002, Hindutva-based fascism used the state apparatus to orchestrate a genocide of Muslims. These fascist forces perpetrated unheard of brutalities against men, women, and children (including those in the womb). Protests were mounted against that genocide all over India; women's organizations and organizations led by women spearheaded the protest activities at national, regional, and international levels. It is recognized that fascism in India, as in Bosnia and Kosovo, uses the bodies of women as the markers of ethnicized "honor" and as targets of attack on enemy territory. In India, even though most of the left political formations are still dominated by men, they have had to recognize the struggle for equal rights for women as an integral part of the people's struggles for equality and justice.

All over the third world, people are fighting for their rights over water, land, forests, and livelihood, and local organizations are often born out of the need to carry the fight further. In Cochabamba, Bolivia, workers won a famous fight to prevent a transnational corporation from usurping all the rights of the local residents to water—water for irrigation, water for sanitation, and water for drinking. In India, fishermen have won the right to fish in the Ganga against waterlords trying to monopolize the river's fishing facilities. In struggles scattered across India, many local groups have demanded and obtained the right to govern themselves in most areas of life. In India, a structure of local governance had been in partial operation through a system of municipal corporations and village *panchayats*. But in most states, with the exception of Kerala, Tripura, and West Bengal, in which left parties have continuously or intermittently formed the government, the elections to the panchayats and other local bodies of self-governance were held very irregularly. In fact, in some states they were never held, the bodies being administered by appointees of constituent state governments. The seventy-third and seventy-fourth amendments to the Indian constitution have mandated elections to those bodies and endowed them with extensive local powers, including the planning and implementation of development projects. In Kerala, Tripura, and West Bengal, these bodies have given a new sense of self-government to the local people.

However, just as most states of the third world have been rendered powerless by debt bondage, structural adjustment, and privatization programs, so also these local bodies are being penetrated by the forces of imperialism. The architecture of financial domination by big capital erected by the transnational corporations, the IMF, World Bank, WTO, and G7 powers often remains invisible to grassroots workers until they are hit by the kiloton bombs of the stealth bombers and their lives are totally destroyed. There is an illusion among some activists that the disempowering of the national state is always a good thing. However, in poor countries, it is ultimately only the state which can provide universal primary education, primary health care, basic sanitation, and food security for the poor and protect common property resources. Getting the state to make these provisions is part of the democratic struggle throughout the world.

The state must have adequate financial and administrative resources to carry out this public provisioning function. Most nation-states have been deprived of all financial clout as a result of their indebtedness. Their powers of recovery have been destroyed because creating state enterprises, interfering in markets, and taxing the rich are actions that global capital and its henchmen consider to be beyond the bounds of the state's legitimate authority. In countries in which the state still has adequate financial resources for making the required public provisions, the monetary and fiscal authorities treat all such ventures as criminal waste, so that local bodies are deprived of the funds needed to look after the basic human needs of people under their jurisdiction. With increasing debt burdens and depleting disposable revenues, they must then turn to aid agencies such as the World Bank and its many satraps, the U.S. Agency for International Development or Britain's Department for International Development, for funding projects. As they take up these projects, they inevitably get entangled in their conditionalities. And thus many a left-oriented political authority begins objectively to act as an agent of transnational corporations. The proliferation of foreign-funded NGOs has also hastened this development.

Hence the resistance against the forces of global capital and imperialism needs to be both local and global. People must agitate against the activities of transnational and domestic big capital, against the strengthening of repression and the deliberate exacerbation of regional armed conflicts in the name of defense, and against the operation of undemocratic organizations such as the IMF, the World Bank, and the WTO. At the same time, the anti-imperialist workers must struggle to establish the rights of fishermen to fish in rivers and coastal waters, of Adivasis to local water, plant, and animal resources, of town dwellers to clean water and air, and of children to grow up as fully competent world citizens.

The state-sponsored genocide in Gujarat and the unprovoked, criminal aggression against Iraq by U.S. and British forces have demonstrated that capital will not hesitate to use the entire armory of fascism to achieve its ends and that raising the slogan of "free markets" is no better than calling the aggression against the people of Iraq "Operation Iraqi Freedom." These onslaughts of capitalism-gone-fascist have also demonstrated that the battle, as it ever was, is for the minds of men and women, as well as for control over the means of coercion. Bush and Blair have used the disarray among the governments of developing countries, and especially the disunity among the governments of west Asia and North Africa, to mount their war. In Gujarat, the enfeebling of the workers' struggle in the towns and workplaces provided an opportunity for the Hindutva formations to recruit the poorest and most disadvantaged of the workers into their campaign of extermination against Muslims. Not only have wrongs committed more than a thousand years ago by one particular invader with a professed faith in Islam been invoked by the Hindutva forces, but the actual events in that ancient feud have been embellished, manipulated, and falsified to poison the minds of the Adivasis as well as those of caste Hindus and Dalits. Similarly, in the buildup to the criminal acts of the U.S. and British governments in Afghanistan and Iraq, there have been echoes of the Crusades of the Christians against Muslims and the branding of all Muslims as terrorists.

Fortunately, in India, although some of the established media parroted the Bush-Blair propaganda and the Hindutva lies, there were other major channels which tried to portray the reality belying that propaganda. Alongside the media cacophony, protests against the Gujarat genocide and the carnage in Afghanistan and Iraq have resounded across most cities and regions of India and other countries of South Asia as well. More people than ever before are aware that freedom is endangered by the fascist forces in the United States, Canada, and Britain and their supporters in old imperialist countries such as Portugal and Spain, as well as by those operating in India, and that we have to work very hard to prevent the victory of these forces and preserve the dignity of human beings as creatures with the ability to reason and choose. Resistance lives! As we say in India, *Inqilab Zindabad!*

11

Can U.S. Workers Embrace Anti-imperialism?

BILL FLETCHER JR.

No doubt one is a wretched plebeian harassed by debts
and military service, but, to make up for it,
one is a Roman citizen, one has one's share in the task of ruling
other nations and dictating their laws.

—SIGMUND FREUD, *The Future of an Illusion* (1927)

The period between September 11, 2001, and the invasion of Iraq raised many questions about the psyche of the U.S. public in general and the U.S. working class in particular. The ability of the Bush administration to utilize fear and patriotism to refocus attention away from pressing domestic issues has been astounding. The Republican congressional victories in November 2002 were nearly unprecedented and most likely would not have happened had the focus on Iraq not emerged during the prior summer.

The widespread fear that resulted from the terror attacks on September 11 is understandable. The assault on civilians through the destruction of the World Trade Center and the use of civilian aircraft as weapons were certainly crimes against humanity. However, the ability of the Bush administration to link all sorts of real and perceived threats to the personality of Saddam Hussein (and prior to that, Osama bin Laden), as well as to create what looks like a state of permanent war, has resulted in a situation of perpetual anxiety. It has also enhanced the foundation of a pro-imperial front, presumably representing the U.S. people, against the rest of the world. This front has led many people, including those of good intention, into believing that any and all concerns and disagreements expressed overseas or at home about the objectives of U.S.

foreign policy are without foundation. Instead, it is argued, any and all methods to guarantee "our" security must be entertained, regardless of the cost.

For these reasons, the danger of a domestic police state has risen to levels not seen since the Nixon administration. Additional dangers of a cowboy foreign policy in the interests of strengthening a U.S.-dominated global capitalist empire place the entire planet at risk and certainly do not increase security for anyone.

In this situation, a fundamental question emerges. Can a working-class-based, anti- imperialist movement emerge that shifts U.S. foreign policy and, in the long term, lays the foundation for the transformation of the U.S. state? To answer this question, we must ask ourselves some difficult questions about labor, "race," and empire. It must be said at the outset that much of our focus will be on the organized sector of the U.S. working class, in order to consider the strategic and tactical options for the creation of a new set of politics through a transformation of organized labor.

THE CRISIS OF CONTEMPORARY U.S. LABOR

The defining ideological feature of the modern U.S. labor movement is the Gompersian notion of trade unionism. Samuel Gompers, founder and long-time leader of the American Federation of Labor (AFL), rose out of the Cigarmakers Union in the latter decades of the nineteenth century. Responding to the crisis in the Knights of Labor, a significant and more radically inclusive labor federation, Gompers argued that workers could only be organized effectively on a craft basis. Although he paid lip service to unskilled workers, Gompers's emphasis was on the skilled crafts. In constructing the American Federation of Labor, Gompers built a ruling bloc that supported such a vision and was soon able to surpass the Knights of Labor in size and influence.

Gompers broke with the earlier U.S. tradition, and that of Europeans, in his opposition to a labor party for the working class. This view flowed from his belief that the role of the trade union was to fight in the interests of the workers in the workplace. Further, his philosophy dictated that the trade union movement accept the existence of capitalism and take no steps in opposition to it. Gompers' program came to be known as *bread-and-butter trade unionism* or *job conscious trade unionism*, most notable for its claim to be pragmatic and not ideological. In the political realm, this meant that organized labor would not have permanent friends or enemies; instead it would have permanent interests. At one level, that might sound quite class conscious, but Gompers was not speaking about the entirety of the working class, only its organized, craft-based sector. When it came to political action, Gompers restricted the AFL to lobbying rather than the political mobilization of the working class.

The roots of Gompers's philosophy of trade unionism were in his view of class and the state, and, by implication, race, gender, and U.S. foreign policy. Though once a socialist, he soon rejected any noncapitalist view of the future. The role of trade unionism was to improve the lives of those who were fortunate enough to be in such unions. Gompers was actually embracing a peculiar form of trickle-down thinking; what was won by the trade unions might eventually improve the lives of the unorganized sector. Yet the unorganized sector was not Gompers' concern. If they wanted improvements, they should join or form unions.

Gompers's pragmatism reflected an *exclusionary unionism*, a view that the objective of unionism is to narrow the relevant population to that which can cut the best deal with capital. The AFL, from its beginning, excluded the bulk of unskilled workers, as well as the mass of workers of color and female workers. This "pragmatic" practice demonstrated, in practice, the racism and sexism of the AFL.

Gompers also came to view the U.S. state as essentially an empty vessel that could be filled by any sort of politics or political/economic influence. The job of the trade union movement was to exert pressure on that state to benefit organized labor, and through the trickle- down effect, the whole of the working class. It was not necessary for the working class to challenge the capitalists for state power. The state could be influenced either by organized labor or by capital. It was up to organized labor to ensure the former. The class character of the state was denied by Gompers. For him, the state is a class-neutral entity, a view which holds sway within much of organized labor even today.

Gompers slowly but steadily abandoned any concern about matters of race and gender. After the great 1892 general strike in New Orleans, a strike which demonstrated the potential of a racially united labor movement, the matter of race and its significance declined in importance for him. By the early 1900s, Gompers had become an open white supremacist.

Within Gompers's "pragmatism," it was a short step from the repudiation of class struggle and the fight for power to the open embrace of capitalism and the government's efforts to strengthen U.S. business interests abroad. In other words, there existed a unity for Gompers between labor and capital; both continually sought a better economic climate. In the realm of foreign policy, this view came to mean open, unconditional, and even rabid, support for whatever the U.S. government did abroad. An early example of this was the AFL's embrace of the First World War and its support of the suppression of opponents of the war, such as the Industrial Workers of the World, a left-wing union which had had considerable success organizing workers ignored by the AFL. For Gompers, the interests of organized labor were allied to a strengthening of capitalism and the success of U.S. foreign policy, regardless of the impact on workers in other countries. The flag of an *imperialist* patriotism was to be the banner of the AFL.

Alternative politics challenging Gompersian trade unionism did emerge after the founding of the AFL. The Industrial Workers of the World, organizations allied with the Communist and Socialist parties, independent left and progressive currents, and caucus movements of oppressed nationalities have all significantly influenced both the discourse and practice of U.S. trade unionism. Nevertheless, while this alternative politics was sometimes successful, the Gompersian view (often aided by a repressive state) has remained hegemonic. The reluctance, and frequent opposition, to tackling racist oppression (always with the excuse that this would create divisions); the tailing after the Democratic Party, and worse, the crass currying of favors from both major parties; and the consistent support of U.S. foreign policy in the name of patriotism have continued. And they have, in fact, strangled the development of the movement.

THE "PATRIOTISM" OF ORGANIZED LABOR

To further explore the consequences of organized labor's "pragmatism," we need to examine the notion of *patriotism*. According to the *American Heritage Dictionary of the English Language,* patriotism is "Love of and devotion to one's country." Yet this is not the operative definition of patriotism in U.S. politics. The operative definition is more akin to "support for the policies of one's government irrespective of the social costs, if said policies are justified as being in the interests of the nation-state." In the United States, this operative definition has been used primarily to suppress dissent.

Gompers wrapped organized labor in the operative definition, and the AFL and later the AFL-CIO used it to crush opposition to its pro-business, pro-imperialism policies. Most critically, two decades after Gompers's death, the operational definition was critical when the cold war commenced and loyalty oaths were enacted into law. In the late 1940s, unions representing over one million workers were expelled from the Congress of Industrial Organizations (CIO) for failing to sign affidavits, mandated by the Taft-

Hartley Act, signifying that their leaders were not Communists. In order to justify and enforce these expulsions, "patriotism" was an effective means of intimidating opponents. Linked to this skewed view of patriotism was the notion promoted by the political right that antiracist activity was a sign of communist influence. This became the case within organized labor as well. The unions that were expelled from the CIO were those that had the strongest positions against racism within the labor movement.

The operative definition of patriotism, then, is a call for class collaboration and a repudiation of genuine international working class solidarity. In the realm of international affairs, for instance, the AFL and, after their merger, the AFL-CIO supported foreign policies that accepted U.S. world hegemony and overseas trade union movements which were in opposition to the political left. In other words, the operative definition of patriotism supports the empire; what stands domestically in opposition to the empire is seen as unpatriotic. Organized labor, seeking to justify its own existence and withstand attacks from the capitalists, chose the expedient route of support for, and advancement of, the operative notion of patriotism. It supported policies that were antithetical to working-class interests but which often seemed to be in labor's (and especially labor's leaders') short-term economic interests.

A RACE-NEUTRAL SOCIAL CONTRACT, OR, DOES A RISING TIDE RAISE ALL BOATS?

Established trade unionism embraces the notion of a *social contract* between labor and capital, within the context of the capitalist system. In embracing this conception, however, the leaders and members of organized labor put on blinders when it came to matters of race and gender. Not coincidentally, these blinders also inhibit the ability to see and understand the empire.

It is once again important to clarify terms. The early usage of the term *social contract* derives from the Enlightenment and the U.S. and French Revolutions of the eighteenth century. The term referred to a myth, elaborated by the intellectuals at the service of the emerging bourgeoisie, to the effect that a bond or contract had been implicitly made in the early years of humanity to end prehistoric barbarism. This social contract presumably recognized basic rights for all sectors of society and protected people against arbitrary rule.

While the nascent bourgeoisie used the myth of the social contract in its struggle with absolute monarchies and feudalism, the term, in fact, justified the existence of classes and the relative role for each of them. This was true whether the social contract took the crude Hobbesian form or Rousseau's more revolutionary and egalitarian form.

In the twentieth century, however, the social contract took on a new meaning, particularly in the aftermath of the Great Depression and the Second World War. It came to refer to the welfare state and the demand upon society to protect its citizens. Again, a myth developed that there was a basic acceptance by all sectors of society of the existence of a strong public sector, core social benefits for all, and trade unionism. In reality, there was never full acceptance of these precepts, nor was there ever consistent implementation of the policies which would have made these a reality. There was, however, a balance of forces in the class struggle that gave this new meaning of the social contract some plausibility.

Organized labor has typically seen the terms of the social contract as narrowly economic. Under Gompers's reign, those who were fortunate enough to be in AFL unions were seen as the beneficiaries of the social contract. The fate of those outside official trade unionism was left to chance. Over time, the views within organized labor changed, with a greater concern for the conditions and future of unorganized workers. This took the form of organizing the unorganized, particularly in the 1930s and 1940s, and later within the public sector, during the 1960s and 1970s, as well as fighting for progressive legislation.

Even during the New Deal, the social contract was never consistent. The trade union movement could perpetuate the myth of this contract only by its failure to address racial disparities in the working class and among the oppressed more generally. For example, Roosevelt's agricultural and labor programs overlooked black farmers and farmworkers in the South and Asian and Chicano farmers and farmworkers in the Southwest. Little was done later, during the "golden years" of U.S. capitalism (1945–1973) to address the secondary (low-paid and insecure) labor market situation facing the majority of black and Latino workers.

The social contract myth assumed that capitalism now had a human face and would be forced to respect all sectors of society. It also assumed that the conditions for the existing workforce would continually improve so that the living standard of their children and grandchildren would always be better. This myth was a white myth. Racial differentials in jobs, housing, education, and health policies always militated against the full implementation of the social contract.

The existence of a relative privilege for whites over people of color created a myopia that reinforced the social contract myth. The ability to rise from the poverty of the early years of immigration led many whites to believe that this society was and remains equitable in its treatment of its citizens. The social contract promised the continuance of this modus vivendi. Indeed, the racial nature of the social contract permitted the transformation of Europeans into white people.

In addition to its racial character, the social contract myth also had an imperial quality. The great wealth of the United States was not simply the result of domestic economic performance and ingenuity, but also of its global power. By the end of the Second World War, the United States was the premier capitalist-imperialist power, and the dollar was the de facto international currency. The United States has used its international power to export its debt, gaining badly needed cash resources to sustain its economic stability. This imperial role, therefore, did not have solely a psychological impact on U.S. workers (and not just whites); it also had a positive material impact on the condition of the bulk of the U.S. working class and petty bourgeoisie. Defending this status quo became for many an essential component of the theory and practice of their lives and their organizations.

Yet the racial and imperial nature of the social contract myth and the failure of organized labor to challenge it undermined the ability of workers to conceive of themselves as having any legitimate and independent progressive class interests. One of the most tragic examples of this took place following the Second World War, when the trade union movement failed in its effort to conduct a large-scale Southern organizing effort (known as Operation Dixie) and subsequently failed to integrate itself into the emerging civil rights movement. The bulk of organized labor, though bloodied by the defeat of Operation Dixie and the subsequent passage of the rabidly antilabor Taft–Hartley Act, believed that it nevertheless had an established place in the tripartite relationship of business, government, and organized labor, a place which dictated that labor promote U.S. capitalism.

A second tragedy revolved around the open support of U.S. foreign policy, even when that foreign policy took direct aim at workers overseas. Examples range from support for the crushing of French dockworkers in the late 1940s, and for military coups in what was then British Guiana in 1964, and Chile in 1973. Despite the known impact of such actions on the working classes of these countries, the bulk of organized labor was prepared to serve as foot soldiers in the fight to promote U.S. interests. In its anticommunist crusade, organized labor could generally be counted upon to disrupt and attempt to destroy legitimate working-class organizations, including those in Brazil during the 1980s (the Central Unica dos Trabalhadores or CUT), as well as those in South Africa in the late 1980s and early 1990s (the Congress of South African Trade Unions or COSATU).

The impact of the racial social contract myth on labor has become particularly critical in the last twenty-five years, with the collapse of the welfare state–New Deal consensus and its liberal conception of the social contract. Had the collapse of the welfare state and the social contract only affected people of color, organized labor would still be facing a crisis, but a crisis very different from the one it is currently experiencing. Majority acceptance of the equitable nature of the U.S. imperial state would persist, at least to some degree. What is creating a larger crisis, however, is that the emergence of neoliberal globalization, guided by the U.S. imperial state, has challenged the earlier notions of a racial deal for white workers.

A CHALLENGE EMERGES: RIGHT-WING POPULISM

Key to the complicity of most of the white working class, and most significantly its organized component, with U.S. racism and imperialism was a combination of two essential factors: white racial privilege (and the social bloc that it created) and the promise of improving living standards. These two factors, though related, have to be distinguished. White racial privilege is not necessarily tied to the economic strength of the U.S. state. The privilege is fundamentally political and structural and refers to the enforced racial differential between whites and nonwhites in U.S. society. This differential exists in both boom times and depressions, but it is enforced through the practices of both the state and civil society. It can be seen in the areas of employment, education, housing, health, and culture, as well as in arenas where there is a high preponderance of people of color, such as entertainment and sports.

Living standards, on the other hand, correlate with the overall economic picture, the racial differential, and the status of the United States as the dominant imperialist power. Political decisions play a part in living standards, but the performance of the economy is directly affected by larger forces. The stagnation of the U.S. economy, which began in the early 1970s, was driven by economic and political factors. Specific political and economic decisions were taken to deal with this stagnation, and these affected the working class as a whole, usually with a disproportionate suffering within communities of color.

The stagnating economy generated a significant drop in living standards for the bulk of the U.S. working class, and this sent reverberations throughout the entire society. At the same time, the victories of the social movements of people of color and women, as well as changes in immigration patterns, changed the tapestry of U.S. society. It took some time for people to grasp that living standards had permanently declined, but certainly during the 1980s and 1990s this came to be understood. By the 1990s, the established media were giving heightened attention to this phenomenon and its impact on social sectors that had typically thought of themselves as impervious to economic decline.

One of the consequences of declining working-class standards has been the rise of right- wing populism, not just in the United States but in most of the advanced capitalist nations. Its rise in the United States must be understood in terms of the crisis to the white racial bloc, which has unfolded at the same time that neoliberal globalization has arisen.

The challenge to the white racial bloc arose from both the victories in the antiracist struggle and changes in imperialism itself. The victories in the domestic antiracist struggle have resulted in new and unprecedented roles for individuals of color. The appointment of people like Condoleezza Rice and Colin Powell represented a fundamental change at the top levels of power. These are not the traditional roles occupied by people of color, in either a Democratic or a Republican administration. In corporate America, the rise of black CEOs in key companies, such as American Express, is also significant.

The problem created for white America by these developments is summed up in the notorious comment by sports commentator Jimmy "the Greek" Snyder, who bemoaned the future of white players with the advent of black quarterbacks. What happens to the hopes of the average white person? Does it pay to be white anymore?

As a result of both the state and corporate onslaught on labor, which included the wholesale destruction of much of U.S. manufacturing, and the constitution of closer inter- capitalist and inter-imperialist alliances, the U.S. workforce holds no special place for U.S. capital, other than its role as consumer. The threat of movement overseas, not to mention its actuality, has presented a major crisis of confidence in the status quo for the average worker. The loyalty that workers were led to expect from their employers simply does not exist. The loyalty is, as it always has been, to the almighty dollar.

The sense of betrayal goes to the core of contemporary right-wing populism. Despite his poor showings in the 2000 election, political commentator Pat Buchanan summed up the feelings of millions when he launched tirades at the allegedly traitorous companies that had abandoned the "American worker." Buchanan's subtle anti-Semitism, racism, and nativism became the lens for his anticorporate (though certainly not anticapitalist) polemic.

The racial deal is now in shambles. Key elements of the white racial bloc sense betrayal, and white workers (as well as sections of the white petty bourgeoisie) cannot count on improved lives for their children. Thus, a combination of the objective economic decline in the living standards of the average worker and the readjustment in the racial deal has fueled right-wing populism. The anger that this has spawned, whether in the extreme form of the militia movements or in the more acceptable form of a Pat Buchanan, has become a pulsating pressure point within the U.S. social formation.

This right-wing populism is demanding a reinstatement of the white racial deal. Even in its most militant anticorporatism, it is not challenging capitalism but demanding a return to the mythical social contract. With regard to the international situation, at some moments this right- wing populism is isolationist and protectionist, while at others it is expansionist and jingoist. In both cases, however, protection of the U.S. state and its hegemonic role in the world are key: the United States first, and within the United States, so-called natives, and among the so-called natives, whites. Patriotism, in its *operative definition*, then comes to mean defense of the empire against any and all potential threats.

Within the U.S. left, there have at various points been assumptions that the economic decline of the United States, and specifically the decline in the conditions for its working class, would engender a militant if not radical response. This may end up being true, but not quite in the manner in which the left expected. Declining living standards do not automatically lead to any predictable response. The left is seldom the immediate beneficiary. Any politics predicated on this assumption is a politics destined to destruction.

The additional complicating factor is the matter of the white racial bloc. The declining living standards, understood through the prism of white racism and white racial privilege, can easily be blamed on anyone other than the capitalists and the capitalist system. As we have seen over the last twenty years, the growing number of immigrants from the global South, whether documented or not, can be the scapegoats for the unraveling of the "American Dream." Politically this has been in evidence in English-only and anti-immigrant initiatives.

One note should be added here. Right-wing populism does not find the same level of resonance among people of color. Part of the reason for this is obvious in that at the core of right- wing populism in the United States is white racism. Additionally, people of color in the United States have had the "advantage" of seeing the underside of the American Dream. That said, two points are worth making. In the 1990s, with the rise of anti-immigrant sentiment and violence, there was some populist sentiment among segments of communities of color. In the anti- immigrant Proposition 187 campaign in California in the mid-1990s, large numbers, though not a majority, within the African-American, Chicano, and Asian electorates supplemented white fervor in favor of the reactionary proposition. In the competition for limited resources under capitalism, the worst sentiments started to come to the surface. Years later, in the aftermath of September 11, there were calls to variants of right-wing populism within communities of color. In the name of patriotism, African Americans, for example, were called upon to march side by side with others in the United States in the so-called war against terrorism. Many African Americans embraced this call in the hope that we would finally be accepted as "Americans." Things have not quite worked out that way, however.

As already noted, right-wing populism can also serve the interests of imperial expansion, as we have seen post–September 11. Playing into both fear and the desire for revenge, right-wing populism has merged with jingoism to support all sorts of adventures in the name of patriotism, security, and ensuring U.S. hegemony. The desire for revenge, not simply against al-Qaeda but against any group or nation allegedly threatening the American way of life, can play itself out politically as support for war, militarism, and, indeed, political repression. A case in point is the alliance between the reactionary Bush regime and the Teamsters Union under James Hoffa, Jr.

The leadership of organized labor has been relatively paralyzed in addressing the emergence of right-wing populism. Trapped within the Gompersian paradigm, the bulk of organized labor has been unable to respond credibly to the new populism. It has been unable to address the sense of betrayal among many white workers, except rhetorically, due to its lack of deep critique of neoliberal globalization, the lack of a frank admission of the racial nature of the social contract, and the lack of any coherent analysis of U.S. foreign policy. The irony of the current situation is that as we approached the invasion of Iraq, there were sections of the leadership of organized labor that wished to take a stand against the aggression but found that their views were not necessarily mirrored within the membership. This gives new meaning to the notion of reaping what one sows.

The Gompersian paradigm has not only restricted organized labor from addressing race and gender, but it has also inhibited an ability to tackle the picture of global capitalism. Insofar as organized labor saw its role as one of helping to promote a more humane, pro-U.S. global capitalism, it has found itself hamstrung in opposing U.S. foreign policy. Demands for organized labor to face up to its brutal history of support for U.S. imperialism have been met with silence since there is no consensus on this history and whether it was correct to collaborate in these various atrocities. Thus, in the aftermath of September 11, it was nearly impossible to engage in a discussion of U.S. foreign policy and the simmering hatred engendered by the role that the United States has played in the global South. The repression in the name of patriotism that has taken place nationally had its counterpart within the ranks of organized labor when it came to any serious attempt to understand the tragedy of September 11.

CAN ORGANIZED LABOR BE WON TO ANTI-IMPERIALISM?

There is not a clear answer to this question. There are good reasons to believe that segments of the working class, including parts of its organized section, can, in the short run, be won to a variant of anti-imperialist politics. In the long term, anti-imperialism will need to become the dominant view within the U.S. working class if any form of progressive, transformative politics, such as socialism, is to become hegemonic. The Uruguayan writer Eduardo Galeano made the observation that in order for the global South to achieve the level of development that the global North has achieved, there would need to be ten more planets in the solar system. This is a dramatic illustration of the skewed manner in which resources are distributed and used internationally. According to the United Nations, the richest fifth of the world's population consumes 86 percent of all goods and services while the poorest fifth consumes 1.3 percent. In addition to actual resources, wealth is distributed in dramatically unequal fashion as well. Again, according to the United Nations, in 2002 the world's 225 richest individuals, of whom 60 are from the United States, have a combined wealth of over $1 trillion, equal to the annual income of the poorest 47 percent of the world's population.

The imbalance in resources and wealth, a direct result of imperialism, is not referenced here to make a moral appeal. Nor is this an advertisement for the poor starving masses and the charity they need. Rather, in order for the U.S. working class to advance, and specifically in order for the trade union movement to transform itself, an appreciation of this imbalance must become part of the new politics it embraces, for these facts point to what for many people is an unsettling proposition, namely the need for global wealth redistribution.

In order to defeat right-wing populism within the working class and other sectors of U.S. society, a multipronged assault will have to be mounted against points of division. Cracking the white racial bloc and cracking imperial consciousness will be key to that assault. To the extent that segments of the U.S. working class see themselves as victims of the rest of the world, rather than as both pawns and victims in an imperialist game, right-wing populism can be counted on to gain strength.

In this context, the struggle for reparations—both domestically for African Americans and internationally for Africans—has an objectively anti-imperialist character. The demand for reparations begins the discussion about global (and domestic) wealth redistribution. This is not a demand that white people, or in the international context, citizens of the global North, give up their toothbrushes and cars. It is a demand, however, that will necessitate changing the manner in which we live our lives in the global North. It is a demand that will need to be directed at governments, multinational corporations, banks, and the real estate industry for compensation for past atrocities and, in more general terms, reconstruction assistance to place peoples ripped out of history back onto a path of self-determined development.

Again, this is not charity. It is compensation for crimes committed. It is also a recognition that the global North generally, and the people of the United States in particular, cannot be trusted as long as they turn a blind eye to the wealth (and people) stolen from the rest of the world. This may sound moralistic, but it can be put in other terms that are more self-interested: there will be no security for anyone as long as wealth, resources, and power are distributed so unjustly.

Thus, within the organized section of the working class, the struggle for reparations and global wealth redistribution should move from a demand of well-intentioned leftists to becoming a political demand of the movement. Such a demand can take many forms, one being the struggle for a democratic foreign policy.

In light of the Bush administration's codification of the "New World Order" through the release of the new *National Security Strategy of the United States of America* in the fall of 2002, the entire pretense of a peaceful, humane, and harmless U.S. foreign policy has been stripped away. The new doctrine proclaims, for all the world to hear and see, that the United States heads the global capitalist empire; that no other power shall be allowed to contend with U.S. military might; and that the United States reserves the "right" to take preemptive military action against any nation or force that it deems to be a threat to its interests.

While the United States has historically engaged in much of what the new doctrine advocates, what is different is the blatant nature of the proclamation. What is also different is the flagrant disregard for the opinions and actions of the key imperialist allies of the United States, with a case in point being the heated international debate surrounding Iraq. The Bush administration has succeeded like few before it in isolating the United States internationally, and what is striking is the arrogant denial of the importance of this isolation.

Developing anti-imperialism as a mass current within the working class involves a fight for a democratic U.S. foreign policy. Of course, as long as the United States remains an imperialist power, there will always be objective limits to its ability to have a democratic foreign policy. Nevertheless, it is the fight that is critical in changing the consciousness of the U.S. working class with regard to the role of the United States on the world stage. Such a struggle could include demands for reparations and/or reconstruction assistance, massive assistance to the Global AIDS Fund, renunciation of the 2002 National Security Strategy, withdrawal of military assistance from dictatorial regimes, removal of agricultural subsidies from U.S. agribusinesses, full repayment of dues to the United Nations, replacement of the World Trade Organization (WTO) with a democratic, multilateral trade institution, and the list could go on and on. In sum, this is a fight for altering the role of the United States within the international arena.

There is an additional side to the fight for a democratic foreign policy. The engagement of the working class in this struggle represents a strike against the Gompersian dependence on either of the two established capitalist parties. Such a struggle brings to the fore the notion of an independent working-class view of the world rather than tailing after whoever happens to be the "best" Democrat. Trade union policy during the Clinton era demonstrated the bankruptcy of failing to take an independent stand. Even when there were disagreements with Clinton on foreign policy (or domestic policy, such as with welfare reform), there was a deep fear of establishing independent terrain. This made it exceedingly difficult for the union movement to conduct a *consistent* struggle against Clinton's pro-globalization policies (with the exception of the WTO demonstrations).

Another challenge to the U.S. working class is that of protectionism. Protectionism can sometimes appear to be anticorporate, if not anti-imperialist, but it is actually neither. While it is the case that the working class is justified in its anger at the loss of jobs, rather than a protectionist response, there must be a response that strikes at capital and supports workers overseas. As Jesse Jackson so eloquently demanded during his 1988 run for the presidency, there must be accountability—which could be described equally as a form of repair/reparations—on the part of capital when it vacates a neighborhood, community, city, or state.

This matter goes to another issue which extends beyond the scope of this paper. With the loss of many value-producing jobs due to either technological changes or moving offshore, the productivity gains by corporations must be shared. We cannot assume that there will be a return of such high-paying jobs in the future; thus, to borrow from the late Tony Mazzocchi, founder of the Labor Party (of the United States), there will need to be a redefinition of work. There will additionally need to be a massive effort to unionize existing jobs to transform them from low- wage to higher-wage employment.

A second response to the shifting of jobs overseas is true international labor solidarity. The growth of left-led trade union movements in places such as South Africa, Nigeria, Brazil, and South Korea represents a major development in the fight for global justice. Not only has this growth meant an improvement in the living standards of the workers, but it also has made it far more complicated for the capitalists to place workers in what has come to be known as a race to the bottom. The AFL-CIO under John Sweeney has brought about considerable improvements in the arena of international labor solidarity, but it has been inconsistent, with remnants of cold war trade unionism continuing to sneak through. The choice for organized labor in the United States all too often seems to be between the desire for respectability in bourgeois circles with the accompanying fantasy of a return to the "good old days" of the New Deal's social contract, and solidarity with genuine foreign labor and other social movements.

One final arena implicit in the above is opposition to U.S. wars of adventure. While it is conceivable that a scenario analogous to the Second World War might at some point reemerge, there is nothing like that on the horizon. Instead, and in line with the new national security doctrine, we are now witnessing the further militarization of the United States, justified, in the most cynical manner, by alleged concerns about human rights, terrorism, and so-called rogue states. Liberal and progressive forces are constantly placed on the defensive when the political right demands that actions be taken against this or that state. Instead, we must "flip the script," so to speak, and ask the difficult questions as to the objectives of U.S. policy and military actions. To do this, particularly in the post–September 11 environment, fear must be directly addressed. As long as fear of alleged and real threats dominates the national discourse, anti-imperialism will be suppressed.

The fear that most people experience today is uncertainty about further terrorist attacks. This fear has been played upon by the Bush administration and the political right in order to increase militarization and domestic repression, and to discourage any popular examination of the deteriorating

U.S. (and global) economy. This can and will be broken if people come to understand the political nature of the terrorists (both clerical fascists and state terrorists), as well as the actions of the United States which have laid the basis for the sympathy that many of these terrorists receive.

CONCLUDING THOUGHTS

The challenge to the U.S. working class and to organized labor cannot be addressed without some formal left presence. The emergence of anti-imperialism as a current, rather than as a set of politics elaborated by a few individuals, will require sustained engagement in various political struggles, both within the trade union movement and more broadly.

The movement against U.S. aggression in Iraq is precisely the sort of mass social phenomenon which can lay the foundation for an anti-imperialist movement. Even here, though, this will fail unless there is a more organized left presence to tie the various strands together.

Discussion of the reconstitution of such a left goes beyond the scope of this paper. Suffice it to say, though, that the development of genuine anti-imperialism is tied to a vision of a different world. Anti-imperialism in its best sense is not solely a reaction against the atrocities of the global North, but the suggestion that the world can and should operate on a fundamentally different basis. Creating and articulating such a vision should be the task of a genuine left. In the absence of such a left and a new vision, we find ourselves facing and fighting endless resistance battles with little hope of final victory.

12

Prospects for Anti-imperialism: Coming to Terms with Our Own Bourgeoisie

SAM GINDIN

In building an anti-imperialist movement—that is, a movement that can ultimately transform the American empire—we will need all the help we can get from objective contradictions. Increasingly it has seemed that two of the contradictions are potential splits within the global elite and a potential cri sis within the American economy. I'll argue, however, that these are the wrong places to find the main contradictions in the American empire. I'll also suggest that we haven't paid enough attention to the fact that contradictions are themselves not static—in the absence of the political capacities to take advantage of the openings they provide, it is the oppositional movement rather than the social system that might get waylaid. If individuals search for ways to adapt to, rather than change, the realities they face, their responses can negatively affect class formation, popular consciousness, and future political openings.

Our movement, it is commonly stressed, will need to combine the organizational resources and strategic potential of the labor movement with the energy and creativity of the social movements, particularly the new generation of global justice activists. But trying to *stitch* these two movements together is, I'll contend, the wrong way to frame the problem. Finally, our project seems to traverse two distinct planes: our vision is universal and internationalist and the capitalism we face is global in scope, yet class power is reproduced nationally. How do we navigate this apparent paradox?

Let me begin with the splits among the global ruling classes, what used to be called inter- imperial rivalry. By the late 1960s, Europe and Japan had significantly closed the economic gap with the United States and, it seemed, inter-imperial rivalry was a factor again in the global political economy. Military conflict within the capitalist core may have been a thing of the past, but not so for potentially destabilizing tensions within the most developed capitalist countries. History, it appeared, had caught up with Lenin. Furthermore, according to Robert Brenner, the increased economic competition, along with the alleged inflexibility of concentrated and "sunk" capital—fixed and specific capital that has already been paid for—implied overcapacity and depressed profit rates. Brenner's details were questioned, but his argument that this structural crisis has continued into the present was generally accepted.[1]

The problem with this focus on the return of inter-imperial rivalry and the persistence of the crisis of the 1970s is not just that both are empirically wrong, but that they divert us from addressing the *new* contradictions that have emerged directly out of the resolution of the old ones.[2] We need to understand these in terms of the most important development of the postwar period, one that Harry Magdoff had such a commitment to placing on the left's agenda: the creation of the American empire. And we need to understand the current conjuncture in terms of the reconstitution of that empire in the 1980s and 1990s.

The postwar reconstruction of a liberal order under American leadership created the dense institutional networks among the developed capitalist countries that in fact tended to eliminate any prospects for inter-imperial rivalry. The very process through which Japan, and especially Europe, subsequently narrowed the economic gap with the United States included their penetration by American capital and the American state, and their tight integration into the American-led world order. By the late 1960s Europe and Japan had reached a point in their development that justified raising the renegotiation of the terms of American dominance, but there was by then no question of challenging the *fact* of that dominance, never mind withdrawing from its reach. "The question for them," as Nikos Poulantzas put it in the early 1970s, "is rather to reorganize a hegemony that they still accept. . . . What the battle is actually over is the share of the cake."[3] When the United States closed the gold window in 1971, what some saw as a sign of weakness was clearly grasped as quite the opposite by a *New York Times* reporter: "In breaking the link between the dollar and gold . . . the United States has shown who is Gulliver and who the Lilliputians."[4]

Nevertheless, the American-led capitalist world order did indeed stumble through the 1970s. But once the American state finally accepted the need for structural adjustment within the United States itself (as when Federal Reserve chairman Paul Volcker restricted the money supply, slowing inflation and growth), this initiated the neoliberal restructuring of labor, capital, finance, internal state structures, and global relationships that restored American economic vitality and reconstituted American power. The conditions of the golden age, as the quarter- century of rapid growth after the Second World War has been called, had reinforced working- class expectations, and workers had used their union and political power to make significant gains. But those democratically achieved gains had become a barrier to accumulation; neoliberalism was the set of policies and institutional changes—rooted in the relations of power embedded in markets—launched to reverse those gains. The concurrent development of financial markets at home and above all internationally, deepened the neoliberal project.

Unlike the earlier retreat from the convertibility of the dollar into gold which spoke only to American defensiveness and its own direct self-interest, neoliberalism evolved to address the more general needs of *global* capital. Neoliberalism spoke to strengthening the disciplinary logic of capitalism within *each* social formation, serving as a potentially universal model for other countries as well as a vehicle for consolidating the national and international conditions for moving toward a world of seamless accumulation—that is, globalization.

These successes (successes, that is, from capital's perspective) brought a special dimension of complexity to the emerging world order. The American state was dominant but not omnipotent; it could only rule through other states. Though these states, especially those at the capitalist core, had come to accept responsibility for reproducing the conditions for international accumulation within their own borders, they remained distinct centers of accumulation that continued to be responsive to domestic social forces. Those states that were oriented to globalization but unable to impose conditions conducive to global accumulation—primarily the former colonies of the European empires—posed more difficult problems. States outside the globalization process—particularly those like Iraq that also had a degree of independence based on oil—might ultimately only be restructured and "brought in" through direct intervention. This fact of ruling through states that are themselves extremely uneven in their capacities (consequently evincing wide variations in their degree of internal stability) and also operating in the context of economies differentially integrated globally introduces complications to empire that create serious problems for global management.

Moreover, the fact of ruling via neoliberalism, with its own unevenness, its hyper- competition and volatility, adds to that complexity. This was notably the case in the third world where neoliberalism as a strategy for initiating *development*—as opposed to a policy for enforcing discipline within already developed capitalist economies—has generally failed to create the conditions for stable capital accumulation. In the neoliberal world that subsequently evolved, crises and instabilities were no longer periodic tendencies but became aspects of global capitalism's *regular functioning*. As an economic adviser to the Bank for International Settlements (BIS) so delicately put it, "Over the last 20 years or so, there seems to have been a continuous series of financial incidents meriting the attention of public policymakers."[5] Crises of one sort or another are now an expected and even necessary part of the system's dynamism, and central bankers have identified the issue as containing, rather than preventing, them.[6]

To date, capitalism has shown a remarkable proficiency in localizing, and limiting in duration and depth, the steady stream of such crises. Whether or not the American state, along with other states and international institutions, can indefinitely continue to manage this increasingly complex system is an open question. Given the political space and time to learn from past experience, to experiment, and to develop new institutional capacities, we see no definitive contradiction that makes the kind of breakdown that 1929 represented inevitable. The issue therefore reverts to the strength of the oppositional movement: Can it develop the capacities to deny global capitalism that necessary political space and time to get its act together?

In this regard, the same factors that account for the complexity also create the material and ideological openings that might create that resistance. I emphasize *openings* to stress that the actual contradictions of empire are *soft*—political opportunities more than intimations of imminent collapse.

- The American empire, in part because it rules through other states, has only achieved sporadic and conditional popular legitimacy outside the United States.
- The restructuring of third world states via the intervention of the IMF and the World Bank has not only had limited developmental success but has invited comparisons to colonial interventions.
- The existence of American capital within each social formation, and the outward orientation of so-called national capital, undermine the authority of the domestic capitalist class to speak in the national interest.
- Neoliberal globalization also tends to undermine, or at least weaken, the capacities of states to legitimate capitalism itself: the earlier promises of steady material security and growing equality have given way to the demands of competitive insecurity; that of growing control over our lives has been trumped by the requirements of expanded accumulation; free trade agreements expose the centrality of consitutionalizing and guaranteeing property rights over all other rights.

Yet in the absence of an effectively organized opposition with a larger vision, the potential to build on such openings will be lost. The danger is that the legitimacy that was formerly bought through progressive change is achieved at less expense through fatalism. Wages may be restrained, but families looking to maintain their consumption can increase the number of hours they work (more family members in the workforce, more hours per member) and increase their debt. This not only creates additional pressures and hardships; it also impacts on class consciousness and class formation, affecting potential resistance in the future. A working class that sustains its living standards through family members working longer hours will be different than a class that wins higher wages on the picket line. A working class that accepts the loss of social programs and goes into debt to replace them privately—and then supports tax cuts so it can pay for the services the state no longer provides—will be different than a class that looks to political mobilization to introduce and expand social entitlements.

And though, with the internationalization of production, workers may no longer accept that what is good for General Motors (or Northern Telecom) is necessarily good for the United States (or Canada), this has not led to a challenge to the concept of competitiveness; rather, the issue has been reformulated as the necessity for creating nationally competitive spaces independent of the nationality of the investment attracted. As a result workers, by accepting and conforming to the law of value as expressed through global competition, contribute to the internationalization of accumulation at the same time that they are integrated into a narrowly nationalistic project of exporting unemployment elsewhere.[7]

Unions, it must be said, have both reflected and contributed to this impasse. Absent a larger politics, economic militancy gets exhausted, many labor leaders gravitate to the relatively more comfortable world of limited possibilities and therefore limited pressures from below, and unions shift defensively inward. In the early 1990s it seemed that an effective working-class response to a decade of neoliberalism was emerging. Social democracy began to win elections again, first in Canada (Ontario) then in Europe, but social democracy proved incapable of addressing a world in which options had been radically polarized. By the mid-90s, partly in response to the frustrations with formal politics, workers in France, South Korea, Canada, and elsewhere were taking to the streets in massive and creative protests, yet there was no sense of how to sustain this opposition or where to take it.

It might seem that the energy, organizational creativity, moral optimism, and global vision of the global justice movement is precisely what a disoriented labor movement now desperately needs to get moving again. But this ignores particular weaknesses in important sections of the global justice movement itself. For example, to the extent that the enemy is identified as *bad* corporations, we tend to take as our aim a world populated by *good* capitalists that only engage in *normal* exploitation. To the extent that the target is mean-spirited international institutions, what is passed over is that ending the IMF and WTO would only mean that third world countries would have to turn to bilateral loans from private banks or foreign governments; they would still face the same, if less institutionalized, pressures to get their priorities in line if they want to attract investors or get access to first world markets. As tactics, this kind of politics has certainly led to impressive degrees of mobilization, yet—as some within the movement have increasingly been arguing themselves—it falls far short of a socially transformative politics.

Bringing the labor movement and the global justice movement together would of course be a good thing. But we should not exaggerate what is achieved when two movements, neither of which has yet developed a strategic orientation for dealing with global capitalism, come together. Nor should we underestimate the extent to which these movements can even be joined without radical transformations—cultural revolutions—inside each of them.

For the labor movement such a transformation means coming to see its members as more than *just* workers and discovering the potentials of unions as centers of working-class life. It is only on the basis of such approaches to their members and institutions that unions can contribute to building the political capacities of their members and can play a leading role in mobilizing broader communities. For the antiglobalization movement this means coming to understand that they can only sustain themselves and grow by grounding themselves in domestic struggles without losing their sensitivity to the international. Moving in this direction would include rethinking how the movement understands the world, how it organizes, how it identifies the issues, where it locates the site of politics. It would, for example, mean that the movement ask itself why it can get fifty to a hundred thousand people out to a demonstration against the WTO but not against domestic racism, homelessness, or lost jobs.

In the *Communist Manifesto*, Marx asserted that our struggles are inherently international in "substance" by virtue of their interrelatedness, "yet in form, the struggle of the proletariat with the bourgeoisie is at first a national struggle. The proletariat of each country must, of course, first of all settle matters with its own bourgeoisie."[8] Accumulation may be global but markets, classes, and property rights are reproduced *nationally*. Social transformation consequently demands that we ultimately come to terms with the power of the nation-state.

The global justice movement has, for many good reasons, rightly been suspicious of the danger of such a statist politics, while the working class has, all too readily, looked to a state it believed only needed better leaders to do good things for them. The point, however, is not to capture the state but to transform it into an instrument that embodies a new kind of democracy—one that contributes to the development of our capacities to participate and is central to mobilizing popular power. This is itself not the end of our ambitions, but a moment in the democratic transformation of the economy, a step toward gaining control over all aspects of our lives and collective potentials, and in positioning ourselves to contribute more concretely to the transfer of resources and technology to the third world implicit in any valid notion of social justice.

The emphasis on the need ultimately to address state power at home does not, however, mean the postponement of concerns with international solidarity until later. Not only are mobilizations at home against the American empire and supports for particular struggles abroad fundamental to our universalist sensibility, but every domestic struggle expands the space for other domestic struggles and each of these struggles includes the most valuable experiences that struggles everywhere must share and study. Moreover, while for those of us outside the United States, anti-imperialist mobilization will underline the need for a de-linking from the American empire, for those who remain within the belly of the beast nothing can be more important than developing an internationalism that counters and begins to neutralize the jingoism of empire.

In this regard, third world struggles urgently need radical stirrings in the first world in order to gain the space and support to be successful. In spite of capitalism's destructive failures in the third world, and in spite of the impressive resistance that has occurred, the beginnings of change *there* are conditional on at least a heightening of the struggle *here*. The crisis in Southeast Asia has, at least for now, proved functional to global capital rather than a threat to it. In Argentina, the total breakdown of the economy may have left a legacy of anger and organizational skills for the future, but for now a *normality* of a kind seems to be returning with the reelection of the Peronists. Global capital seems relatively confident that it can contain the election of Lula through Brazil's global financial linkages. And in Africa, the problem is as often as not identified as the continent's marginalization from, rather than the form of its historic integration into, the global economy.

Prospects for an anti-imperialist struggle do not, in short, revolve around simply adding up the forces we already have, or solemn commitments to try harder. In the first world, we need a left that locates itself within both the labor movement and the other movements, while seeing this bridging of the two as part of the project of transforming each. And in order to both help ourselves and contribute to third world struggles, we must come to understand the old issue of state power in a new and internationalist way.

13

Notes on the Antiwar Movement

BARBARA EPSTEIN

The movement against the war in Iraq was the largest antiwar movement ever. Even in the United States, where opposition to the war was not as large as in many other parts of the world, demonstrations against the war grew with astonishing rapidity. Before the war began, demonstrations had reached sizes that, during the war in Vietnam, had taken years of organizing to mobilize. The antiwar movement, in the United States as elsewhere, was also in many respects quite broad. It included not only people on the left, antiglobalization activists, and peace groups, but also churches, other religious organizations, trade unions, and many other organizations not associated with the left. And it included very large numbers of people who came to demonstrations as individuals, rather than as members of organizations, and who had never before participated in a political protest.

The movement against the war in Iraq was also international to a degree that no other antiwar movement has ever been. Opposition to the war in Vietnam took place in many countries, but it was centered in the United States; the antiwar movement in the United States tended to overshadow antiwar movements elsewhere. This time not only was the opposition to the war outside the United States of extraordinary proportions but the movement as a whole understood itself as an international movement, to the extent that protests came to be internationally coordinated. The international character of the antiwar movement helps to account for one of the differences between the movement against the war in Iraq and the movement against the first Gulf War, in 1991. At that time there was strong protest until the war began; when public opinion in the United States turned decisively in favor of the war, the antiwar movement collapsed. This time protest was sustained well into the war. The strength of international protest was no doubt an important factor in sustaining protest inside the

United States, even as the media and public opinion were shifting toward unquestioning support of the war.

Another strength of the antiwar movement was the sophistication of its perspective, especially in comparison with earlier antiwar movements. Those who opposed the war in Vietnam were divided over its causes. Many who opposed the war believed that it was an aberration, a mistake on the part of a particular group in power. Even on the left, among those who argued that the war was part of a social system, those who were willing to call that system imperialism were in a small minority. The concept of imperialism was so identified with the far left that many who believed that the war grew out of an imperialist system avoided using the word. After the war in Vietnam the use of the word *imperialism* remained very unpopular even on the left. But in the current antiwar movement, understanding of the war in Iraq as imperialist has been very widespread. This is partly because there are some on the right who are now openly defending a policy of imperialism. But it also reflects a widespread understanding in the antiwar movement that the attack on Iraq was one component of a larger agenda of world domination.

Antiwar organizers point out that protest against the war was based on people's understanding of the broad implications of the war. Paul George of the Peninsula Coalition for Peace and Justice brought church and other religious groups together to oppose the war, in the largely middle-class suburbs south of San Francisco. I asked him what drove the people he works with to oppose the war: was it concern about the war's impact on the domestic economy, or fear of terrorist attacks in the United States, or fear of the erosion of democratic rights? He said that the people he worked with opposed the war for all of these reasons and more. The war, he said, went against their basic values. They saw it as a grab for world power, an attack on democratic rights in the United States and abroad, and a danger to the United Nations, to international order, and to world peace. The people he worked with, George said, saw the war in Iraq as the first step in a plan for a widening of U.S. international dominance, which they found frightening and morally abhorrent.

Paul George's account of why people in the antiwar movement opposed the war coincided with the impressions of other antiwar organizers with whom I spoke. Jackie Cabasso of the People's Non-Violent Response Network, a coalition of mostly faith-based antiwar organizations in the Bay Area, and Amy Newell, chair of U.S. Labor against the War, gave me similar accounts of why their constituents opposed the war. These organizers and others argued that most of the people who became involved in the antiwar movement did so out of their conviction that the international ambitions of the Bush administration endanger peace, democratic rights, and prosperity in the United States and abroad. It is taken for granted in the antiwar movement that the Bush administration wants both oil and power, and that the close relationship between the Bush administration and the oil companies is a factor in the administration's actions. There are some in the antiwar movement who would avoid the word "imperialism," but few would quarrel with the view that the Bush administration wants U.S. world dominance, both economic and political.

Previous antiwar movements have been based mostly on opposition to particular wars. Every antiwar movement in the United States in the twentieth century has included small numbers of pacifists who have opposed all war, and, in many cases, larger numbers of socialists, who have opposed capitalism and/or imperialism. But every antiwar movement has been composed mostly of people whose concern was limited to stopping that war. The fact that so many of those who opposed the war in Iraq saw it in broader terms is an enormous advance, and it gives reason to hope that the antiwar movement will be sustained beyond the U.S. victory in Iraq.

Along with these strengths the antiwar movement also had some weaknesses, which need to be examined if we want to sustain opposition to the Bush administration and its ambitions. The most glaring weakness of the movement against the war in Iraq was the limited involvement of people of color, especially African Americans. According to many polls, blacks opposed the war in roughly the percentages in which whites supported it. At one point approximately two- thirds of whites supported the war and approximately two-thirds of blacks opposed it. At other points African-American opposition to the war was even higher. There were African Americans in the antiwar movement and in its leadership; the same was true of other groups of color. But there was a striking contradiction between the racial composition of the antiwar movement and the racial breakdown of opposition to the war.

The whiteness of the antiwar movement is a result of the racial divisions in U.S. society, which are particularly deep between blacks and whites. The depth of these divisions makes it unlikely that large numbers of blacks will be willing to join any predominately white movement, even if they support its aims. Progressive movements with predominantly white membership and/or leadership should do whatever they can to reach out to African Americans and other groups of color and to align themselves with progressive organizations led by people of color. Predominantly white organizations should also examine the internal culture of their movements to see if there are obstacles to the participation of people of color. Efforts along these lines will improve the racial balance of the movement but will not produce miracles. In Oakland, California, a coalition of groups, affiliated with the national organization United for Peace and Justice, organized an antiwar march. Determined that their march would at least to some degree reflect the racial composition of Oakland, they put a great deal of effort into reaching out to local activists of color, publicizing the march in local neighborhoods, and inviting local activists to speak at the rally. These efforts had results: the march included a higher proportion of people of color than the larger, nationally sponsored demonstrations in San Francisco. But if the Oakland march had accurately reflected antiwar sentiment in Oakland, it would have been predominantly African-American. It was not.

It is also important to remember that communities of color have been differentially affected by the increased police repression of the last thirty years. A much smaller proportion of white youth are under correctional supervision on probation or parole. The consequences of a misdemeanor arrest at a demonstration for someone on probation or parole could well be immediate imprisonment.

One of the dangers posed by the racial imbalance of the antiwar movement, and of the movements that are likely to follow it, is that activists will try to address this problem by slinging charges of racism at each other. Among progressives, charges of racism have enormous power; nothing is as likely to destroy an organization or drain the energy out of a campaign than a debate conducted in these terms. The racial imbalance of the antiwar movement is more likely to improve as a result of attention to outreach and to creating an environment within the movement in which people of color as well as whites will feel welcomed and will be treated with respect. Because such efforts are not likely to transform the racial composition of the antiwar movement, it is also important to support autonomous initiatives from communities of color. The self-organization of people of color around anti-imperialist struggles will enhance opportunities for broader coalitions in which people of color will play leading roles.

The antiwar movement was lopsided not only in terms of race but also in terms of age. There were significant numbers of young people in the movement; they brought verve and creativity to demonstrations, and they took the lead in civil disobedience. But the young people in the antiwar movement represented a small minority of their generation. This contrasted sharply with the movement against the war in Vietnam: the majority of activists were young, and the movement was based on the campuses. During the protests against the war in Iraq, U.S. campuses were relatively quiet.

The Vietnam antiwar movement was limited by its identification with youth culture. At that time, many older people who opposed the war had a difficult time finding a place in the movement. The recent antiwar movement was strengthened by the diversity of generations participating in it. But young people play a particularly important role in social movements, and if there had been more of them in the recent antiwar movement, the movement and its prospects would have been strengthened.

One of the reasons for the relatively low level of involvement of young people is the absence of a draft. It is also the case that many young people are reluctant to become involved in political activity. There are practical factors: today's college students have less free time than college students of the 1960s and 70s did. But time is a problem for virtually everyone who wants to engage in political activity. Today's young people grew up in the conservative culture of the last two decades which has promoted individual material success. The young people in the global justice movement reject these values and hold out different ones, but most young people absorb the prevailing values at least to some degree; in today's fiercely competitive environment rejecting these values has a cost. The student and other youth organizations against war that exist should be supported; the antiwar movement, or whatever evolves out of it, should encourage young people to find their own forms of protest and resistance.

In addition to its problems in reaching people of color and young people, the antiwar movement has been organizationally fragile. This antiwar movement emerged out of a near vacuum in the U.S. peace movement and the U.S. left. The peace movement was badly demoralized by the first Gulf War. There was considerable public opposition to that war before it began, but as soon as war was declared much of that opposition evaporated, and within two weeks the antiwar movement had largely collapsed. Over the decade that followed the peace movement languished. On the left, democratic socialist organizations continued a decline that had been taking place for decades. The fall of the Soviet Union, initially seen by some as opening up a space for a more positive version of socialism, in fact further discouraged the left by removing the only major obstacle to the expansion of U.S. corporate power. The major sign of hope for the left came at the end of the decade, with the emergence of an anarchist-oriented global justice movement among young people, which became visible to the public in Seattle in November 1999. This movement, which flourished for more than a year in the United States, suffered a setback as a result of the attack on the Twin Towers on September 11, 2001. Out of concern that any demonstrations could provoke official repression and public hostility, anti- corporate-globalization activists refrained from mobilizing major protests against the Bush administration's attack on Afghanistan.

The organization that stepped into this vacuum was International Act Now to Stop War and End Racism. ANSWER was formed shortly after September 11 by the International Action Center, in which the Workers' World Party played a central role. ANSWER skillfully mobilized demonstrations against the war on Afghanistan, and when the Bush administration began warming up for an attack on Iraq, it was ANSWER that stepped in to mobilize protest. ANSWER was able to do this because it had experience in doing such work and the necessary organizational structure. Members of the Workers' World Party had played a similar role during the first Gulf War. An alternative antiwar coalition, United for Peace and Justice, was formed out of the concern that ANSWER failed to appeal to a broad enough constituency. Both Leslie Cagan, the chair of United for Peace and Justice, and Bill Fletcher Jr., a vice-chair, publicly identified themselves as socialists. These and other socialists in leading positions in the antiwar movement worked with nonsocialists to build a broader movement. Some two hundred religious, labor, and other organizations joined in the coalition formed by United for Peace and Justice, giving it the broad base that ANSWER lacked. On the East Coast, especially in New York, United for Peace and Justice became at least as important a force in the antiwar movement.

The movement against the war in Iraq functioned in an atmosphere of unremitting crisis, contributing to the structural fragility. The movement had two tiers. There were the national coalitions, including ANSWER, United for Peace and Justice, Not in Our Name, MoveOn.org which mobilized against the war over the Internet, and Win Without War, which appealed to a predominantly liberal constituency to the right of the other major national coalitions. Alongside the national coalitions were massive numbers of local organizations that opposed the war. These included peace centers and other peace organizations revived by the ferment of activity against the war in Iraq and groups formed to oppose a war in Iraq. The groups and organizations opposing the war also included innumerable organizations of other types, churches and other religious organizations, trade unions, and social justice organizations that turned at least some of their efforts toward opposing the war. The churches, especially white middle-class churches, probably made up the largest component of this grassroots antiwar movement. The massive participation of such mainstream organizations, especially the participation of so many church groups, in the antiwar movement, gave it enormous credibility.

The problem with the two-tiered structure of the antiwar movement was that neither of the tiers was likely to outlast the crisis surrounding the attack on

Iraq. The national coalitions were really committees of national organizers, who were able to mobilize huge numbers of people to attend demonstrations, or sign statements or contribute money, under conditions of crisis. The vast majority of the local organizations in the grassroots antiwar movement had been formed around issues other than war. Under conditions of crisis, they took time out from their usual concerns to oppose the war. Once the crisis receded, these organizations tended to return to their usual concerns. The sponsorship of antiwar protests by churches, trade unions, and other organizations with which large numbers of people identify no doubt drew people to demonstrations who might not have attended otherwise. But most people who participated in demonstrations went with family or friends, not as members of organized groups. Once the atmosphere of crisis dissipated, there were few avenues for continuing antiwar activity, or even arenas for discussion of what to do next. During the First World War, in the United States the Socialist Party served as a center for antiwar activity. During the War in Vietnam, the Students for a Democratic Society played the same role.

As antiwar activists have pointed out, the war in Iraq was only the first step in the Bush administration's efforts to extend its power. The next steps may not involve hot wars. The leaders of other nations targeted by the United States as enemies may calculate that it is better to accommodate U.S. demands before being attacked. It would be unfortunate if the antiwar movement in the United States were only capable of responding to war or threats of war. In the past, antiwar protest was centered among particular groups (during the 1960s, students and young people, for instance). No single group played this role in relation to the war in Iraq. It is unlikely that any single organization will emerge as the center of ongoing opposition to U.S. imperial ambitions. But if there are no membership organizations for antiwar/anti-imperialist activists, the movement will lurch from crisis to crisis, responding to events of the moment but unable to develop or carry out any long-range strategy.

There was no effort to form ongoing antiwar organizations before or during the war partly because of the sense of impending crisis: at every point it seemed as if war might begin within a week or two, leaving no time for anything but mobilizing the largest demonstrations possible. In a sense the war continues: The United States is now occupying Iraq and growing Iraqi protest will no doubt lead to unforeseen consequences for the United States. The Bush administration is making threatening noises in the direction of various other countries. This is nevertheless a moment of relative calm in which it might be possible to address issues such as the structure of an ongoing antiwar/anti-imperialist movement. It also might be a good idea to point to connections between war and, more broadly, the U.S. drive for empire and other issues.

One of these is the environment, which is endangered on a global scale by the pace at which oil and other natural resources are being used up. Alternative, sustainable sources of energy need to be developed and promoted if we are to stave off an environmental crisis that could assume such proportions that war would look minor in comparison. A second, related issue is the culture of consumerism in the United States. A host of institutional and social pressures push Americans toward expenditures that seem to hold out the promise of a happy family life, security, respect from one's community but which in fact tie most Americans to the longer and longer working hours that undermine family and community. Entrapment in this culture promotes support for empire because it provides access to global resources. The young anarchists make a scathing critique of the culture of consumerism, and some of them try to find ways of living outside it. This probably works better for young people, especially those with middle-class family resources to fall back upon when necessary, than for other sections of the population. The socialist left might not arrive at the same solutions, but it should begin to prioritize the issue, because it is connected to the widening gap of wealth and power between the United States and the rest of the world.

The antiwar movement, if it is to gain strength and momentum, needs to link up with the broader global justice movement, and the global justice movement needs to link its labor and environmental segments more effectively. To accomplish all of this it is necessary to draw out the connections between production and consumption under capitalism—by way of the critique of commodity fetishism. There should be no war for oil but also no war for the auto-petroleum complex and no war for the system of production and consumption that makes such patterns of accumulation necessary. Until such connections are drawn, the movement will lack staying power, the capacity for its different elements to coalesce, and a meaningful political praxis.

14

Construction of an Enemy

ELEANOR STEIN

Remember the Nazi technique: "Pit race against race, religion against religion, prejudice against prejudice. Divide and conquer!"

—PRESIDENT FRANKLIN D. ROOSEVELT, in January 1942, admonishing Americans not to discriminate against aliens, weeks before he signed the Japanese exclusion order.[1]

The aggressive measures instituted by the Bush administration against immigrants and visitors of Muslim faith or from primarily Muslim Arab and South Asian countries seem aimed less at their putative foreign targets than at the hearts and minds of our domestic population. Packaged as post-September 11 law enforcement, the new racial profiling has netted few if any prosecutions for terrorist acts but has done a great deal to demonize Arabs, South Asians, and Muslims, to dehumanize them, and to construct them as the enemy of the United States in the twenty-first century. Once the state successfully constructs an enemy group, it can justify detentions without charge, military occupation, and other drastic means of waging war against that other, the enemy.

Nativist and xenophobic identification of immigrants with national security threats is a theme coincident with the history of the United States. The Naturalization Act of 1790 prohibited citizenship and civil rights to immigrants of disfavored ethnicity. The Alien and Sedition acts of 1798 placed restrictions on which ethnicities or nationalities could apply for citizenship and authorized the president to order the deportation of all immigrants judged dangerous to national security. The "sedition" of concern in 1798 was the ideas of the French Revolution. The Chinese Exclusion (Geary) Act of 1882, in violation of the express terms of a treaty in force between China and the United States, forbade Chinese laborers from entering the United States.

The National Origins Act of 1924 established immigration quotas privileging "Nordic" immigrants. The Smith Act of 1940 required registration and fingerprinting of aliens and added vague classifications of "subversives" and "excludables" to the list of deportable persons. The McCarran–Walter Act of 1952 empowered the Department of Justice to deport immigrants and naturalized citizens engaging in "subversive" activities. The Anti-Terrorism and Effective Death Penalty Act of 1996 granted the executive the authority, based upon secret evidence, to designate any foreign organization a terrorist group and to deport noncitizens as terrorists.

But it was the internment of Japanese Americans during the Second World War that elevated xenophobia into national policy. And it was in the internment cases that the Supreme Court, upholding the internment as a matter of military necessity, wrote the requirement of strict judicial scrutiny of "invidious" distinction into American jurisprudence.

Based upon reports by the military that it had intercepted radio and light signals between offshore locations and the California coast, the evacuation and internment orders forced persons of Japanese descent to leave their homes in specified control areas in California, Arizona, Oregon, and Washington and move to internment camps. Over 120,000 persons, two-thirds of them U.S.-born citizens, spent the years of the war in such camps.

The internment order was rationalized not only by military necessity—the fear of sabotage and espionage—but also by the military's claim that the normal criminal investigatory work of the Justice Department had been overly slow and inadequate to guarantee U.S. security. The racist hysteria in which the roundups took place was fed by the Hearst press and by California economic interests—such as the White American Nurserymen—in competition with small entrepreneurs of Japanese descent.

Two brave individuals, Fred Korematsu and Gordon Hirabayashi, refused to report for internment and sought to challenge the order in the federal courts. In a shameful decision, the U.S. Supreme Court upheld as constitutional this mass internment. Forty years later, when the two whose refusal to report for internment had led to Supreme Court cases sought (and received) judicial exoneration, it was discovered that the military report that was the justification for the internment order and the Supreme Court decision was a complete fabrication. An archival researcher, working in conjunction with a congressional commission appointed to investigate the internment, found the original report. The intercepted radio and light signals, dutifully repeated in the Supreme Court opinion, had never occurred.

The shadow of Manzanar—the California interment camp—looms today over all of the current measures being taken against Arab and Muslim immigrants. These measures can be seen as internment for the twenty-first century—or to coin a more accurate term, externment.

Shortly after September 11, 2001, the "Ashcroft Raids" occurred, the secret detention and deportation of a thousand or more Arab or Muslim men. Some were held for months, even as long as one year, without access to lawyers and, in some cases, to families. Ashcroft stated he intended to jail every terrorist he could find, and that net included thousands of Muslim noncitizens. What were the results of this dragnet? Not a single person charged with involvement in the September 11 attacks, and four indicted on charges of support for terrorism, with none of the indictments including any specific violent acts. The Justice Department now admits that at least 766 persons were detained on "special interest" charges after September 11 and held incommunicado; of these, 511 have been deported. The Justice Department claims that among those deported were some who could have been—*but have not been*—charged with terrorism offenses. This in turn has led to speculation that one purpose of the mass detention policy was the recruitment of intelligence agents[2]. An additional six thousand were deported for violations of immigration status. Eight thousand were called for interviews on the sole ground that they were recent male immigrants from Arab countries.

The USA Patriot Act, enacted within six weeks of September 11, permits the Attorney General to detain noncitizens without a hearing and to bar foreign citizens from entering the United States on the basis of their political opinions. It also authorizes deportation based upon support of a disfavored group. None of these restrictions is tied to participation in any terrorist act. On April 29, 2003, the Supreme Court approved mandatory detention of "criminal aliens" pending deportation—that is, permanent resident aliens convicted of any of a list of crimes who are subject to deportation have no entitlement to a hearing to consider bail for the period they contest or await deportation.

Coming soon may be Patriot Act II, which modifies the definition of "foreign power" to include all persons, regardless of whether they are affiliated with an international terrorist group, who engage in international terrorism; and defines any person who engages in clandestine intelligence-gathering activities for a foreign power as an agent of that power, regardless of whether those activities are federal crimes.

One of the most far-reaching forms of racial profiling is the requirement of the Immigration and Naturalization Service, now merged into the Office of Homeland Security, termed Special Registration. These new rules apply to any male over the age of sixteen who is not currently a permanent resident (green-card holder), from twenty-five countries: Afghanistan, Algeria, Bahrain, Eritrea, Iran, Iraq, Lebanon, Libya, Morocco, North Korea, Oman, Qatar, Somalia, Sudan, Syria, Tunisia, United Arab Emirates, Yemen, Pakistan, Saudi Arabia, Bangladesh, Egypt, Indonesia, Jordan, and Kuwait. These men were required to register in person at an immigration office during February and March 2003 on a few weeks notice, to be photographed, fingerprinted, and interviewed, in many cases about their political beliefs and associations. More than 125,000 registered; over 2,000 were detained. All must reregister annually and any time they leave the United States. A widespread panic resulted in immigrant communities, and thousands in the New York and New England areas traveled with their families to the Canadian border to seek asylum; however, the United States had closed the border. Hundreds were detained there, their families left without shelter or resources in the bitter New England winter. Local refugee assistance organizations, overwhelmed, were forced to close their doors.

Government profiling also contributed to a wave of popular violence against Arab, South Asian, and Muslim communities. The number of reported U.S. hate crimes against Muslims and Arabs in 2002 increased 1,600 percent over the previous year.

The construction of an enemy, through government targeting with media complicity and a popular echo, endangers and dehumanizes millions of Arabs, Asians, and Muslims. The bombing of Iraq's cities and the sacking of its history were presented on U.S. television as an extreme sport. The construction of an enemy provides an effective means of control of the domestic population, which visits its fears and frustrations on its Arab and Muslim neighbors. This control is, however, contested. Towns and cities all over the country have passed local government resolutions criticizing and even refusing to enforce the Patriot Act.

Fred Korematsu and Gordon Hirabayashi waited forty years for vindication and reparations; few outside the Japanese-American community, with the notable exception of the Quakers, had opposed internment. Hopefully, we are doing better this time. Interfaith groups are building bridges to Muslim communities. In upstate New York, Women Against War organized a toy drive for children of detainees and deportees to celebrate Eid, the end of Ramadan and, with national civil liberties organizations, recruited attorneys and other volunteers to assist men reporting for Special Registration and their families. And shortly after September 11 the National Asian Pacific American Legal Consortium invited Arab Americans to join them at the

National Japanese American Memorial to show solidarity in anticipation of racial profiling. Resistance, as ever, is based on acts of individual decency, which in these sad times appear as acts of courage. But the liberty interests of all U.S. residents are implicated; if we do not stand by our Muslim neighbors in their registration, detention, and deportation nightmare, we will have a yet harder time when these techniques are more widely applied.

15

Homeland Imperialism: Fear and Resistance

BERNARDINE DOHRN

The creation and cultivation of fear is one of the pillars of empire both abroad and within the imperial "homeland." And that fear is always accompanied by the threat of discipline, punishment, and violence. Every state uses violence to enforce its power against its enemies, but we must recognize that a major change has occurred. September 11, 2001, gave a green light for a full-blown and bipartisan agenda of repression at home, as well as for the expanded imperial project abroad.

Yet it is important when we talk of repression always to pair it with resistance. As we pile up the evidence of consolidated state power, we must remember that a part of what has happened since 9/11 includes 2/15—that is February 15, 2003, when as many as ten million people around the world simultaneously joined to cry out against U.S. imperialism.

This robust and unified resistance to imperialism is indeed new, but in the United States and elsewhere, it did not come from thin air. On the local level, on the person-to-person level, incredible organizing work has been underway, focused on prisons, women's health and safety, labor, the environment, reparations, global justice, solidarity with Latin American and African countries, and human rights movements. Anti-death-penalty struggles have, notably in my home state of Illinois, begun to achieve great things.

These social movements and organizing from below are invisible to the U.S. newspapers and CNN, but they are the cauldron in which people understand the connections between issues and come to understand reality. And so as we talk about the cultivation of fear and repression, we should note that what looks strong is also weak. The message sent by the U.S. mass media is not necessarily the message received.

Miles Horton founded the Highlander Center in 1938, in its time a center for adult organizing and education throughout the South, and indeed throughout the country. He often told a simple little story. In the mid-1960s, the Klan put up a series of billboards across the South with a famous picture of Martin Luther King Jr. at Highlander. It showed several people from the Communist Party, as well as King and Rosa Parks, sitting in the front row of a lecture. It had a circle around Dr. King's head and the caption "Martin Luther King at Communist training school."

Miles described going with a carload of young teenagers to a civil rights demonstration in the South, and as they passed one billboard nobody in the car said anything. As they passed a second one somebody in the back said, "Hmmm." And when they passed a third one, a kid in the back seat said, "You know, that's the dumbest poster I've ever seen, because they don't tell you who to call." The powers that be think they're giving one message, but it's actually being received in other ways.

The scope of the current repression is vast, and as separate resistances are created it is our task to unite them. There's no detail too small for repression at this moment. Under attack are state medical marijuana statutes (an attack initiated by the Clinton administration), end of life statutes in Oregon, abortion, the judiciary, environmental protections, social security, public education, women's rights, and a range of progressive measures from birth control to OSHA regulations. Far-right and neoconservative cultural activists are assigned to each of these domains to implement a reactionary plan that has been articulated since 1964. A part of their strategy includes the culture wars and the criminalizing of the 60s.

The heart of today's repression is the American addiction to caging African-American people, especially young men. This is the model for the cage in which the United States now seeks to place the entire world. The mass incarceration of people of color took place through a very deliberate cultivation of fear, the legend of a crime wave, and the invention of the superpredator myth during a decade when crime rates plummeted. Key facts about the United States are that prison construction and staffing has become the largest sector of state budgets, the fastest growing major on college campuses is criminal justice, and the fastest growing union has been the union of prison guards. When Angela Davis speaks of the "prison industrial complex," she's not kidding. It has become a major set piece of economic, social, and cultural life, and at its core is the caging of young African-American men, overwhelmingly for nonviolent offenses.

How has this happened? The field was well prepared in U.S. history, but it was sown with the development of fear promoted on the nightly news, the anxiety that strangers were coming through your window, the imagery of young kids shooting each other and shooting up high schools, and the conviction that this was likely to happen in your neighborhood, although all the facts were to the contrary.

And so the legacy of slavery, the modern-day version of slavery, is reflected one way in prisons but it is also visible in the transformation of schools. Schools in America have become barricaded places of fear. People who do not have their own youngsters in school today may not realize what has happened to the environment where our young people spend seven hours of their day. You can't get into a school and you can't get out. Surveillance is pervasive. There are lockdowns, body searches, and dogs. There are armed guards. And all of this is in schools that have never seen a violent incident. The fear of violence and the notion that it is likely to come from anywhere, including from our young people, has been the precursor and the trial run for what is now happening in all of our public spaces and airports.

Now we have war abroad and war at home. The second stage of the process is the silencing. Ari Fleischer, the day after 9/11, proclaimed "beware of what you say" and announced that you're for us or you're against us. The jihad is here, at home, and it's going to be enforced by the neoconservatives; consider the full-page ads that the *New York Times* seems to run once a month from people like William Bennett. Such an ad ("Americans for Victory over Terrorism") states as its purpose: "We will take to task those who 'blame America first.'" The target of this jihad "against terrorism" is the population here at home, and so this notion of "taking to task" means menacing and disciplining, threatening, and silencing people like Susan Sontag, Bill Maher, Danny Glover, and university faculty all over the country. The result is a chilling effect. That is to say, people around the targets back away, get silent, don't stand up when they see the cost of simply expressing an opinion or even making a joke, let alone publicly objecting to what is going on.

The actual tools of repression—the USA Patriot Act and now the bill creating a Department of Homeland Security—were passed in such a way that it took even the lawyers and legislators who passed them weeks to figure out what they had done. The Patriot Act is 348 pages long; it passed two weeks after 9/11. No one even knew what had made it in or out of the Homeland Security Act until the final moment, and still the INS is trying to figure out which of its functions are assigned to which agency.

The Patriot Act created a new federal crime of domestic terrorism. It is important to recognize the broad brush of what now counts as "terrorism." I am part of a children's law center in Chicago. We represent children in court. We have seen this tremendous mushrooming of young students, of course primarily African-American and Latino youth, getting expelled from school for "terroristic" threats. The word alone creates fear. and by now almost anything manages to scare a lot of Americans.

Here is the language from the Homeland Security Act: "Acts dangerous to human life that are a violation of the criminal laws if they appear to be intended to influence the policy of a government by intimidation or coercion." Malevolent prosecutors and judges (and we do not lack for them) could sweep anything under such language. "Acts dangerous to human life" might be read to include attempting to block any street on which there is vehicular traffic. And think for a moment of the phrase "appear to be intended to influence." The tools are in place to criminalize, as domestic terrorism, basic protests and civil disobedience. Can you doubt that they had Seattle in 1999 in mind?

Prosecutions are underway that are reminiscent of the indictments of the McCarthy period of the early 1950s and the conspiracy indictments of the pre-Watergate Mitchell Department of Justice in the early 1970s—the two most recent periods of overtly political repression. For example, John Ashcroft has orchestrated a series of high-profile indictments against Islamic charities, including the Holy Land Foundation in Texas and the Benevolent Association in Chicago. In the Chicago case Ashcroft flew in to announce the indictments. A year later all the terrorist charges were dropped and the head of the organization pled to one corruption charge, involving improper reporting of received funds. It will not surprise you that the television coverage of the indictment was hysterical, but coverage of the plea quite restrained. The aim was to accustom the U.S. public to, and intimidate the judiciary from interfering with, the repression of freedom of association, and they are no doubt pleased with the results.

Now one must look abroad, or at least as far as Guantanamo, to see the full extent of what is in the works. What were accepted restraints on U.S. power for decades have been shattered. We are talking of torture and extra-judicial executions or assassinations. We have now had the example of the United States executing people on the soil of a state at peace with the United States with no evidence, no charges, and no legal process whatsoever. Torture, like slavery, is practically the only thing in international law and human rights that is an absolute. There are no exceptions to it. Torture is banned; every country in the world has signed on. But we have Guantanamo. We have U.S. troops and CIA forces implementing "stress and duress tactics" as they call them, and we have the U.S. openly admitting to handing prisoners over to be tortured by other cooperating states. This too has not appeared out of thin air; the techniques developed in the last twenty years in "control units" in maxi-maxi prisons in the United States have perhaps paved the way to Guantanamo.

So the long and short of it is that our task is to keep on organizing politically. The structures of opposition are there. We need to make the connections between these issues so that people better understand state power and don't see imperialism as only an optional foreign policy. On the human scale, it's essential to stand up in solidarity. I don't think you can overestimate how important it is, when someone is under attack, to write them a note, to call them up, to object, to stand up and say that you disagree and you think they're acting courageously. That stuff matters. The failure to do it gets noted, and where support is expressed it is powerful.

A friend and colleague at the university has been passing around a poster that he made on a xerox machine. It's a faded picture of four aging Native Americans at the turn of the century in their indigenous dress. They're all holding rifles and they're not posing. They are standing with their rifles looking directly into the camera. And the banner across it says "homeland security, fighting terrorism since 1492." That is our tradition.

16

The New Age of Imperialism

JOHN BELLAMY FOSTER

Imperialism is meant to serve the needs of a ruling class much more than those of a nation. It has nothing to do with democracy. Perhaps for that reason it has often been characterized as a parasitic phenomenon—even by critics as astute as John Hobson in his 1902 classic, *Imperialism: A Study*.[1] And from there it is unfortunately all too easy to slide into the crude notion that imperialist expansion is simply a product of powerful groups of individuals who have hijacked a nation's foreign policy to serve their own narrow ends.

Numerous critics of the current expansion of the American empire—both on the U.S. left and in Europe—now argue that the United States under the administration of George W. Bush has been taken over by a neo-conservative cabal, led by such figures as Paul Wolfowitz (deputy secretary of defense), Lewis Libby (the vice president's chief of staff), and Richard Perle (of the Defense Policy Board). This cabal is said to have the strong backing of Secretary of Defense Rumsfeld and Vice President Cheney, and, through them, President Bush. The rise to prominence of the neoconservative hegemonists within the administration is thought to have been brought on by the undemocratic 2000 election, in which the Supreme Court appointed Bush as president, and by the terrorist attacks of September 11, 2001, which suddenly enlarged the national security state. All of this has contributed, we are told, to a unilateralist and belligerent foreign policy at odds with the historic U.S. role in the world. As the *Economist* magazine framed this issue: "So has a cabal taken over the foreign policy of the most powerful country in the world? Is a tiny group of ideologues using undue power to intervene in the internal affairs of other countries, create an empire, trash international law—and damn the consequences?"[2]

The *Economist*'s own answer was "Not really." Rightly rejecting the cabal theory, it argued instead that "the neo-cons are part of a broader movement" and that a "near-consensus [among U.S. policy elites] is found around the notion that America should use its power vigorously to reshape the world." But what is missing from the *Economist* and from all such mainstream discussions is the recognition that imperialism in this case, as always, is not simply a *policy* but a *systematic reality* arising from the very nature of capitalist development. The historical changes in imperialism, associated with the rise of what has been called a "unipolar world," defy any attempt to reduce current developments to the misguided ambitions of a few powerful individuals. It is therefore necessary to address the historical underpinnings of the new age of U.S. imperialism, including both its deeper causes and the particular actors that are helping to shape its present path.

THE AGE OF IMPERIALISM

The question of whether the United States in engaging in imperialist expansion has allowed itself to become prey to the particular whims of those at society's political helm is not a new one. Harry Magdoff addressed this thesis on the very first page of his 1969 book *The Age of Imperialism: The Economics of U.S. Foreign Policy*—a work that can be said to have reintroduced the systematic study of imperialism in the United States.[3] "Is the [Vietnam] war part of a more general and consistent scheme of United States external policies," he asked, "or is it an aberration of a particular group of men in power?" The answer of course was that although there were particular individuals in power who were spearheading this process, it reflected deep-seated tendencies within U.S. foreign policy that had roots in capitalism itself. In what was to emerge as the most important account of American imperialism in the 1960s, Magdoff set about uncovering the underlying economic, political, and military forces governing U.S. foreign policy.

The ruling explanation at the time of the Vietnam War was that the United States was engaged in the war to "contain" Communism—and hence the war itself had nothing to do with imperialism. But the scale and ferocity of the war seemed to belie any attempt to explain it in terms of mere containment, since neither the Soviet Union nor China had shown any global expansionary tendencies and third world revolutions were obviously indigenous affairs.[4] Magdoff rejected both the dominant tendency in the United States to see U.S. interventions in the third world as a product of the cold war, and the liberal penchant to see the war as an aberration of a Texan president and the advisers surrounding him. Instead historical analysis was required.

The imperialism of the late nineteenth and early twentieth centuries was distinguished mainly by two features: (1) the breakdown in British hegemony, and (2) the growth of monopoly capitalism, or a capitalism dominated by large firms, resulting from the concentration and centralization of production. Beyond these features that distinguished what Lenin referred to as the stage of imperialism (which he said could be described in its "briefest possible definition" as "the monopoly stage of capitalism"), there are a number of other elements that have to be considered. Capitalism is of course a system uniquely determined by a drive to accumulate, which accepts no bounds to its expansion. Capitalism is on the one hand an expanding world economy characterized by a process that we now call globalization, while on the other hand it is divided politically into numerous competing nation-states. Further, the system is polarized at every level into center and periphery. From its beginning in the sixteenth and seventeenth centuries, and even more so in the monopoly stage, capital within each nation-state at the center of the system is driven by a need to control access to raw materials and labor at the periphery. In the monopoly stage of capitalism, moreover, nation-states and their corporations strive to keep as much of the world economy as possible open to their own investments, though not necessarily to those of their competitors. This competition over spheres of accumulation creates a scramble for control of various parts of the periphery, the most famous example of which was the scramble for Africa in the late-nineteenth century, in which all of the Western European powers of the day took part.

Imperialism continued to evolve beyond this classic phase, which ended with the Second World War and the subsequent decolonization movement, and in the 1950s and 1960s a later phase presented its own historically specific characteristics. The most important of these was the United States replacing British hegemony over the capitalist world economy. The other was the existence of the Soviet Union, creating space for revolutionary movements in the third world and helping to bring the leading capitalist powers into a cold war military alliance reinforcing U.S. hegemony. The United States utilized its hegemonic position to establish the Bretton Woods institutions—the General Agreement on Tariffs and Trade, the International Monetary Fund, and the World Bank—with the intention of consolidating the economic control exercised by the center states, and the United States in particular, over the periphery and hence the entire world market.

In Magdoff's conception, the existence of U.S. hegemony did not bring to an end the competition between capitalist states. Hegemony was always understood by realistic analysts as historically transitory, despite the constant references to the "American century." The uneven development of capitalism meant continual inter-imperialist rivalry, even if it was somewhat hidden at times. "Antagonism between unevenly developing industrial centers," he wrote, "is the hub of the imperialist wheel."[5]

U.S. militarism, which in this analysis went hand in hand with its imperial role, was not simply or even mainly a product of the cold war competition with the Soviet Union, by which it was conditioned. Militarism had deeper roots in the need of the United States, as the hegemonic power of the capitalist world economy, to keep the doors open for foreign investment, by force if necessary. At the same time, the United States was employing its power where possible to advance the needs of its own corporations—as for example in Latin America where its dominance was unquestioned by other great powers. Not only did the United States exercise this military role on numerous occasions throughout the periphery in the post–Second World War period, but it was also able to justify this role as part of the fight against Communism. Militarism, associated with this role as global hegemon and alliance-leader, came to permeate all aspects of accumulation in the United States, so that the term "military industrial complex," introduced by Eisenhower in his farewell address as president, was an understatement. Already in his day there was no major center of accumulation in the United States that was not also a major center of military production. Military production helped prop up the entire economic edifice in the United States and was a factor holding off economic stagnation.

In mapping contemporary imperialism, Magdoff's analysis provided evidence demonstrating how directly beneficial imperialism was to capital within the core of the system (showing, for example, that earnings on U.S. foreign investments, as a percentage of all after-tax profits on operations of domestic nonfinancial corporations, had risen from about 10 percent in 1950 to 22 percent in 1964). The siphoning of surplus from the periphery (and misuse of what surplus remained due to distorted peripheral class relations characteristic of imperial dependencies) was a major factor in perpetuating underdevelopment. Unique and less noticed, however, were two other aspects of Magdoff's assessment: a warning regarding the growing third world debt trap and an in-depth treatment of the expanding global role of banks and finance capital in general. It wasn't until the early 1980s that an understanding of the third world debt trap really surfaced when Brazil, Mexico, and other so-called new industrializing economies were suddenly revealed to be in default. And the full significance of the financialization of the global economy did not really dawn on most observers of imperialism until late in the 1980s.

In this systematic historical approach to the subject of imperialism, as depicted above all by Magdoff, U.S. military interventions in places like Iran, Guatemala, Lebanon, Vietnam, and the Dominican Republic, were not about "protecting U.S. citizens" or fighting the expansion of the Communist bloc. Rather they belonged to the larger phenomenon of imperialism in all of its historical complexity and to the U.S. role as the hegemonic power of the capitalist world. However, this interpretation was directly opposed by liberal critics of the Vietnam War writing at the time, who sometimes acknowledged that the United States had been engaged in the expansion of its empire, but saw this, in line with the whole history of the United States, as a case of accident rather than design (as defenders of the British Empire had argued before them). American foreign policy, they insisted, was motivated primarily by idealism rather than material interests. The Vietnam War itself was explained away by many of these same liberal critics as the result of "poor political intelligence" on the part of powerful policy makers, who had taken the nation off course. In 1971, Robert W. Tucker, professor of American foreign policy at the School of Advanced International Studies at Johns Hopkins University, wrote *The Radical Left and American Foreign Policy*, in which he argued that the "saving grace" for the United States in Vietnam was the "essentially disinterested character" with which it approached the war.[6] Tucker's perspective was that of a liberal opponent of the war who nonetheless rejected radical interpretations of U.S. militarism and imperialism.

Tucker's main targets in his book were William Appleman Williams, Gabriel Kolko, and Harry Magdoff. Magdoff was attacked specifically for arguing that control of raw materials on a global basis was crucial to U.S. corporations and the U.S. state that served them. Tucker went so far as to claim that the error of Magdoff's view was shown where the issue of oil arose. If the United States were truly imperialist in its orientation to third world resources, he argued, it would attempt to control Persian Gulf oil. Defying both logic and history, Tucker declared that this was not the case. As he put it:

> Given the radical view, one would expect that here [in the Middle East], if anywhere, American policy would faithfully reflect economic interests. The reality, as is well known, is otherwise. Apart from the increasing and successful pressures oil countries have employed to increase their royalty and tax income (pressures which have not provoked any notable countermeasures), the American government has contributed to the steady deterioration of the favorable position American oil companies once enjoyed in

> the Middle East. A *New York Times* correspondent, John M. Lee, writes: "The remarkable thing to many observers is that the oil companies and oil considerations have had such little influence in American foreign policy toward Israel."[7]

The case of Persian Gulf oil, then, according to Tucker, disproved Magdoff's insistence on the importance of controlling raw materials to the operation of U.S. imperialism. The U.S. political commitment to Israel was counter to its economic interests but had overridden all concerns of U.S. capitalism with respect to Middle East oil. Today it is hardly necessary to emphasize how absurd this contention was. Not only has the United States repeatedly intervened militarily in the Middle East, beginning with Iran in 1953, but it has also continually sought to promote its control over oil and the interests of its oil corporations in the region. Israel, which the U.S. has armed to the teeth and which has been allowed to develop hundreds of nuclear weapons, has long been part of this strategy of controlling the region. From the first, the U.S. role in the Middle East has been openly imperialistic, geared to maintaining control over the region's oil resources. Only an analysis that reduced economics to commodity prices and royalty income while ignoring the political and military shaping of economic relations—not to mention the flows of both oil and profits—could result in such obvious errors.

THE NEW AGE OF IMPERIALISM

Nothing, in fact, so reveals the new age of imperialism as the expansion of the U.S. Empire in the critical oil regions of the Middle East and the Caspian Sea basin. U.S. power in the Persian Gulf was limited throughout the cold war years as a result of the Soviet presence. The Iranian Revolution of 1979, to which the United States was seemingly helpless to respond, was the greatest defeat of U.S. imperialism (which had relied on the Shah of Iran as a secure base in the region) since the Vietnam War. Indeed, prior to 1989 and the breakup of the Soviet bloc, a major U.S. war in the region would have been almost completely unthinkable. This left U.S. dominance in the region significantly constrained. The 1991 Gulf War, which was carried out by the United States with Soviet acquiescence, thus marked the beginning of a new age of U.S. imperialism and expansion of U.S. global power. It is no mere accident that the weakening of the Soviet Union led almost immediately to a full-scale U.S. military intervention in the region that was the key to controlling world oil, the most critical global resource, and thus crucial to any strategy of global domination.

It is essential to understand that in 1991 when the Gulf War occurred the Soviet Union was greatly weakened and subservient to U.S. policy. *But it was not yet dead* (that was to occur later that year) and there was still the possibility, although dim, of a coup or upset and a turnaround in Soviet affairs unfavorable to U.S. interests. At the same time the United States was still in a position where it had lost economic ground to some of its main competitors, and hence there was a widespread sense that its economic hegemony had seriously declined, limiting its course of action. Although the administration of George H. W. Bush declared a "New World Order," no one knew what this meant. The collapse of the Soviet bloc had been so sudden that the U.S. ruling class and the foreign policy elites were unsure of how to proceed.

During the first Gulf War the U.S. elites were split. Some believed that the U.S. should go on and invade Iraq, as the *Wall Street Journal* advised at the time. Others thought that an invasion and occupation of Iraq was not feasible. Over the course of the next decade the dominant topic of discussion in U.S. foreign policy, as witnessed, for example, by the Council on Foreign Relations publication, *Foreign Affairs*, was how to exploit the United States' position as the sole superpower. Discussions of unipolarity (a term introduced by the neoconservative pundit Charles Krauthammer in 1991) and unilateralism were soon coupled with open discussions on U.S. primacy, hegemony, empire, and even imperialism. Moreover, as the decade wore on, the arguments in favor of the United States exercising an imperial role became more and more pervasive and concrete. Such issues were discussed from the beginning of the new era not in terms of ends but in terms of efficacy. A particularly noteworthy example of the call for a new imperialism could be found in an influential book entitled *The Imperial Temptation*, again by Robert W. Tucker, along with David C. Hendrickson, published by the Council on Foreign Relations in 1992. As Tucker and Hendrickson forthrightly explained,

> The United States is today the dominant military power in the world. In the reach and effectiveness of its military forces, America compares favorably with some of the greatest empires known to history. Rome reached barely beyond the compass of the Mediterranean, whereas Napoleon could not break out into the Atlantic and went to defeat in the vast Russian spaces. During the height of the so-called Pax Britannica, when the Royal Navy ruled the seas, Bismarck remarked that if the British army landed on the Prussian coast he would have it arrested by the local police. The United States has an altogether more formidable collection of forces than its predecessors among the world's great powers. It has global reach. It possesses the most technologically

> advanced arms, commanded by professionals skilled in the art of war. It can transport powerful continental armies over oceanic distances. Its historic adversaries are in retreat, broken by internal discord.
>
> Under these circumstances, an age-old temptation—the imperial temptation—may prove compelling for the United States. . . . The nation is not likely to be attracted to the visions of empire that animated colonial powers of the past; it may well find attractive, however, a vision that enables the nation to assume an imperial role without fulfilling the classic duties of imperial rule.[8]

The "imperial temptation," these authors made clear, was to be resisted less because it would constitute a renewal of classic imperialism, but because the United States was only willing to go half way, unleashing its military force while neglecting to take on the more burdensome responsibilities of nation building associated with imperial rule.

Proceeding from a nation-building perspective reminiscent of Kennedy-style cold war liberalism, but also attractive to some neoconservatives, Tucker and Hendrickson presented the case that the United States, having fought the Gulf War, should have immediately proceeded to invade, occupy, and pacify Iraq, removing the Ba'ath Party from power, thus exercising its imperial responsibility. "The overwhelming display of military power," they wrote, "would have provided the United States with time to form and recognize a provisional Iraqi government consisting of individuals committed to a broadly liberal platform. . . . Though such a government would undoubtedly have been accused of being an American puppet, there are good reasons for thinking that it might have acquired considerable legitimacy. It would have enjoyed access, under UN supervision, to Iraq's oil revenues, which surely would have won it considerable support from the Iraqi people."[9]

Tucker and Hendrickson—in spite of Tucker's argument against Magdoff decades earlier, that the failure to seize control of Persian Gulf oil was evidence that the United States was not an imperialist power—were under no illusions about why an occupation of Iraq would be in U.S. strategic interest, in one word: "oil." "There is no other commodity," they wrote, "that has the crucial significance of oil; there is no parallel to the dependence of developed and developing economies on the energy resources of the Gulf; these resources are concentrated in an area that remains relatively inaccessible and highly unstable, and possession of oil affords an unparalleled financial base whereby an expansionist developing power may hope to realize its aggressive ambitions."[10] The need for the United States to achieve domination over the Middle East was therefore not in doubt. If it resorted to force under these exceptional conditions, it should do so responsibly—by extending its rule as well.

This argument comes out of the liberal rather than conservative (or neoconservative) side of the U.S. foreign policy establishment and ruling-class discussions. The debate within the establishment is narrow, with many liberal foreign policy analysts, because of their penchant for nation building, much closer to neoconservatives and more hawkish in this respect than many conservatives. For Tucker and Hendrickson imperialism is a matter of choice made by policy makers; it is a mere "imperial temptation." It could be resisted, but if it is not, then it is necessary to take on the liberal dream of nation building—to reengineer societies on liberal principles.

Indeed, a remarkable consensus on underlying assumptions and goals emerged within the U.S. power elite in the 1990s. As Richard N. Haass, a member of the National Security Council in the administration of President George H. W. Bush and the official who drafted the elder Bush's most important statement on U.S. military posture, observed in the 1994 edition of his book *Intervention*, "Liberated from the danger that military action will lead to confrontation with a rival superpower, the United States is now more free to intervene." In accounting for the limitations of U.S. power Haass declared, "the United States can do anything, just not everything."[11] He went on to discuss the possibility of nation-building interventions in Iraq and elsewhere. Another book by Haass, *The Reluctant Sheriff*, published in 1997, referred to the sheriff and his posse, with the sheriff defined as the United States and the posse as a "coalition of the willing."[12] The sheriff and the posse need not worry too much about the law, he noted, but must nonetheless be wary of crossing over into vigilantism.

More important, was his argument on hegemony, which pointed directly to the main differences within the establishment on the U.S. assertion of global power. According to Haass, the United States clearly was the "hegemon" in the sense of having global primacy, but permanent hegemony as an object of foreign policy was a dangerous illusion. In March 1992, a draft of the *Defense Planning Guidance*, also known as the "Pentagon Paper," was leaked to the press. This secret working document authored by the elder Bush's Defense Department under the supervision of Paul Wolfowitz (then undersecretary for policy) declared, "Our strategy [after the fall of the Soviet Union] must now refocus on precluding the emergence of any potential future global competitor."[13] Questioning this strategy in *The Reluctant Sheriff*, Haass claimed that it was ill conceived for the simple reason that the United States did not have the capacity to prevent new global powers from emerging. Such powers emerge along with the growth of their material resources; great economic powers will inevitably have the capacity to become great powers generally (along a full spectrum), and the extent to which they emerge as full military powers "will depend mostly on their own perception of national interests, threats, political culture, and economic strength."[14] The only rational long-term strategy, since the perpetuation of hegemony or primacy was impossible, was what Madeleine Albright termed "assertive multilateralism" or what Haass himself termed a "sheriff and posse" approach, the posse consisting mainly of the other major states.

By November 2000, just before he was hired to be head of policy planning in Colin Powell's State Department in the administration of President George W. Bush, Haass delivered a paper called "Imperial America" that urged the United States to fashion an "imperial foreign policy" that makes use of its "surplus of power" to "extend its control" across the face of the globe. While still denying that lasting hegemony was possible, Haass declared that the United States should use the exceptional opportunity that it now enjoyed to reshape the world in order to enhance its global strategic assets. This meant military interventions around the world. "Imperial understretch, not overstretch," he argued, "appears to be the greater danger of the two."[15] By 2002, Haass, speaking for an administration preparing to invade Iraq, was pronouncing that a failed state, unable to control terrorism within its own territory, had lost "the normal advantages of sovereignty, including the right to be left alone inside [its] own territory. Other governments, including the U.S., gain the right to intervene. In the case of terrorism this can even lead to a right of preventative, or preemptory, self-defense."[16]

In September 2000, two months before Haass presented his "Imperial America" paper, the neoconservative Project for the New American Century had issued a report entitled *Rebuilding America's Defenses*, drawn up at the request of Dick Cheney, Donald Rumsfeld, Paul Wolfowitz, George W. Bush's younger brother Jeb, and Lewis Libby. The report declared that "at present the United States faces no global rival. America's grand strategy should aim to preserve and extend this advantageous position as far into the future as possible." The main strategic goal of the United States in the twenty-first century was to "preserve *Pax Americana*." To achieve this it was necessary to expand the "American security perimeter" by establishing new "overseas bases" and forward operations throughout the world. On the question of the Persian Gulf, *Rebuilding America's Defenses* was no less explicit: "The United States has for decades sought to play a more permanent role in Gulf regional security. While the unresolved conflict with Iraq provides the immediate justification, the need for a substantial American force presence in the Gulf transcends the issue of the regime of Saddam Hussein."[17]

Even before September 11, therefore, the ruling class and its foreign policy elites (including those outside neoconservative circles) had moved toward an explicit policy of expanding the American empire, taking full advantage of what was regarded as the limited window brought on by the demise of the Soviet Union—before new rivals of scale could arise. The 1990s saw the U.S. economy, despite the slowdown in the growth trend, advance more rapidly than that of Europe and Japan. This was particularly the case in the bubble years of the latter half of the 1990s. The Yugoslavian civil wars meanwhile demonstrated that Europe was unable to act militarily without the United States.

By the end of the 1990s, discussions of U.S. empire and imperialism cropped up not so much on the left as in liberal and neoconservative circles, where imperial ambitions were openly proclaimed.[18] Following September 11, 2001, the disposition to carry out massive military interventions to promote the expansion of U.S. power, in which the United States would once again put its "boots on the ground," as neoconservative pundit Max Boot expressed it in his book on early U.S. imperialist wars *The Savage Wars of Peace*, became part of the dominant ruling class consensus.[19] The administration's *National Security Strategy* statement, transmitted to Congress in September 2002, promoted the principle of preemptive attacks against potential enemies: "The United States must and will maintain the capability to defeat any attempt by an enemy . . . to impose its will on the United States, our allies, or our friends. . . . Our forces will be strong enough to dissuade potential adversaries from pursuing a military build-up in the hope of surpassing, or equaling, the power of the United States."[20]

In *At War with Ourselves: Why America Is Squandering Its Chance to Build a Better World*, Michael Hirsh, senior editor for *Newsweek*'s Washington bureau, presents the argument of political liberals—that while it is proper for the United States as the hegemonic power to intervene where failed states are concerned, and where its vital strategic interests are at stake, this has to be coupled with nation building and a commitment to broader multilateralism. However, in reality this may only be a "unipolarity . . . well disguised as multipolarity."[21] This is not a debate about whether the United States should extend its empire, but whether the imperial temptation will be accompanied by the assertion of imperial responsibility, in the manner raised by Tucker and Hendrickson. Commenting on nation-building interventions, Hirsh declares, "There is no 'czar' for failed states as there is for homeland security or the war on drugs. Perhaps there should be."[22]

What have been called "nation-building interventions," originally rejected by the Bush administration, are no longer in question. This can be seen in the Council on Foreign Relations report *Iraq: The Day After*, published shortly before the U.S. invasion and addressing nation building in Iraq. One member of the task force that developed that report, James F. Dobbins, director of the Rand Corporation Center for International Security and Defense Policy, served as the Clinton administration's special envoy during the interventions in Somalia, Haiti, Bosnia, and Kosovo and also as special envoy for the Bush II administration following the invasion of Afghanistan. Dobbins, an advocate for "nation-building interventions"—the diplomacy of the sword—in both the Clinton and Bush administrations, declared definitively in the report: "The partisan debate over nation-building is over. Administrations of both parties are clearly prepared to use American military forces to reform rogue states and repair broken societies."[23]

THE CABAL THEORY AND IMPERIAL REALITIES

All of this relates to the question that Magdoff raised more than a third of a century ago in *The Age of Imperialism* and that is with us more than ever today. "Is the [Vietnam] war," he asked, "part of a more general and consistent scheme of United States external policies or is it an aberration of a particular group of men in power?" There is now agreement within the establishment that objective forces and security requirements are driving U.S. expansionism, that it is in the general interest of the high command of U.S. capitalism to extend its control over the world—as far and for as long as possible. As the Project for the New American Century puts it, it is necessary to seize the "unipolar moment."[24]

The wider left's tendency over the last two years to focus on this new imperialist expansion as a neoconservative project involving a small sector of the ruling class not reaching beyond the right wing of the Republican Party—resting on particular expansive interests in the military and oil sectors—is a dangerous illusion. At present there is no serious split within the U.S. oligarchy or the foreign policy establishment, though these will undoubtedly develop as a result of failures down the road. There is no cabal, but a consensus rooted in ruling class needs and the dynamics of imperialism.

There are divisions, however, between the United States and other leading states—intercapitalist rivalry remains the hub of the imperialist wheel.

How could it be otherwise when the United States is trying to establish itself as the surrogate world government in a global imperial order? Although the United States is attempting to reassert its hegemonic position in the world, it remains far weaker economically, relative to other leading capitalist states, than it was at the beginning of the post–Second World War period. "In the late 1940s, when the United States produced 50 percent of the world's gross national product (GNP)," James Dobbins wrote in *Iraq: The Day After*, "it was able to perform those tasks [of military intervention and nation-building] more or less on its own. In the 1990s, in the aftermath of the Cold War, America was able to lead much broader coalitions and thereby share the burden of nation building much more widely. The United States cannot afford and does not need to go it alone in building a free Iraq. It will secure broader participation, however, only if it pays attention to the lessons of the 1990s as well as those of the 1940s."[25] In other words, with a stagnating U.S. economy that, despite relative economic gains in the late 1990s, is in a much weaker position vis-à-vis its main competitors than in the years following the Second World War, outright hegemonism is beyond its means, and it remains dependent on "coalitions of the willing."

At the same time, it is clear that in the present period of global hegemonic imperialism the United States is geared above all to expanding its imperial power to whatever extent possible and subordinating the rest of the capitalist world to its interests. The Persian Gulf and the Caspian Sea basin represent not only the bulk of world petroleum reserves, but also a rapidly increasing proportion of total reserves, as high production rates diminish reserves elsewhere. This has provided much of the stimulus for the United States to gain greater control of these resources—at the expense of its present and potential rivals. But U.S. imperial ambitions do not end there, since they are driven by economic ambitions that know no bounds. As Harry Magdoff noted in the closing pages of *The Age of Imperialism* in 1969, "It is the professed goal" of U.S. multinational corporations "to control as large a share of the world market as they do of the United States market." And this hunger for foreign markets persists today. Florida-based Wackenhut Corrections Corporation has won prison privatization contracts in Australia, the United Kingdom, South Africa, Canada, New Zealand, and the Netherlands Antilles.[26] Promotion of U.S. corporate interests abroad is one of the primary responsibilities of the U.S. state. Consider the cases of Monsanto and genetically modified food, Microsoft and intellectual property, Bechtel and the war on Iraq. It would be impossible to exaggerate how dangerous this dual expansionism of U.S. corporations and the U.S. state is to the world at large. As István Mészáros has observed, the U.S. attempt to seize global control, which is inherent in the workings of capitalism and imperialism, now threatens humanity with the "extreme violent rule of the whole world by one hegemonic imperialist country on a permanent basis . . . an absurd and unsustainable way of running the world order."[27]

This new age of U.S. imperialism will generate its own contradictions, among them attempts by other major powers to assert their influence, resorting to similar belligerent means, and all sorts of strategies by weaker states and non-state actors to engage in "asymmetric" forms of warfare. Given the unprecedented destructiveness of contemporary weapons, which are diffused ever more widely, the consequences for the population of the world could well be devastating beyond anything ever before witnessed. Rather than generating a new Pax Americana, the United States may be paving the way to new global holocausts.

The greatest hope in these dire circumstances lies in a rising tide of revolt from below, both in the United States and globally. The growth of the global justice movement, which dominated the world stage for nearly two years following the events in Seattle in November 1999, was succeeded in February 2003 by the largest global wave of antiwar protests in human history. Never before has the world's population risen up so quickly and in such massive numbers in the attempt to stop an imperialist war. The new age of imperialism is also a new age of revolt. The Vietnam Syndrome, which has so worried the strategic planners of the imperial order for decades, now seems not only to have left a deep legacy within the United States but also to have been coupled this time around with an Empire Syndrome on a much more global scale—something that no one really expected. This more than anything else makes it clear that the strategy of the American ruling class to expand the American Empire cannot possibly succeed in the long run and will prove to be its own—we hope not the world's—undoing.

CONTRIBUTORS

SAMIR AMIN is director of the Third World Forum in Dakar, Senegal. His recent books include *Specters of Capitalism: A Critique of Current Intellectual Fashions* (Monthly Review Press, 1998) and *The Liberal Virus: Permanent War and the Americanization of the World* (Monthly Review Press, 2004).

AMIYA KUMAR BAGCHI is director of the Institute of Development Studies in Kolkota, India, and is the author of *Capital and Labour Redefined* (Anthem Press, 2002) and *The Political Economy of Underdevelopment* (Cambridge University Press, 1982).

DAVID BARSAMIAN is founder and director of Alternative Radio (www.alternativeradio.org). He and Noam Chomsky have done a series of interview books. Their latest is *Propaganda and the Public Mind* (South End Press, 2001).

NOAM CHOMSKY, longtime political activist, writer, and professor of linguistics at MIT, is author of numerous books and articles on the media, U.S. foreign policy, international affairs, and human rights. His latest books are *Power and Terror* (Seven Stories Press, 2003) and *Middle East Illusions* (Rowman & Littlefield Publishers, 2003).

BERNARDINE DOHRN, activist, academic, and child advocate, is director of the Children and Family Justice Center and clinical associate professor of law at Northwestern University in Chicago.

ROXANNE DUNBAR-ORTIZ is a longtime activist, university professor, and writer. In addition to numerous scholarly books and articles, she has published two historical memoirs, *Red Dirt: Growing Up Okie* (Verso, 1997) and *Outlaw Woman: A Memoir of the War Years, 1960–1975* (City Lights, 2002) and is working on a third, *Norther: Re-Covering Nicaragua*, about the 1980s contra war against the Sandinistas.

BARBARA EPSTEIN teaches in the History of Consciousness program at the University of California at Santa Cruz. Along with Marcy Darnovsky and Richard Flacks, she is editor of *Cultural Politics and Social Movements* (Temple University Press, 1995). She is a director of the Monthly Review Foundation.

BILL FLETCHER JR. is a longtime labor movement activist who currently serves as the president of TransAfrica Forum, a Washington, D.C.- based nonprofit organizing and educational center formed to raise awareness in the United States about issues facing the nations and peoples of Africa, the Caribbean, and Latin America. He is a director of the Monthly Review Foundation.

JOHN BELLAMY FOSTER is a co-editor of *Monthly Review* and professor of sociology at the University of Oregon. Among his many books are *Ecology against Capitalism* (Monthly Review Press, 2002) and *Marx's Ecology* (Monthly Review Press, 2000).

SAM GINDIN holds the Packer Chair in Social Science in the Department of Political Science at York University in Toronto. He was, for many years, director of research and assistant to the president of the Canadian Auto Workers.

PETER GOWAN is an editor of *New Left Review* and professor of international relations at Metropolitan University in London. He is the author of *The Global Gamble: Washington's Faustian Bid for World Dominance* (Verso, 1999).

JOSEPH HALEVI teaches political economy at the Universities of Sydney, Australia, and Grenoble, France.

MICHAEL KLARE is professor of peace and world security studies at Hampshire College in Amherst, Massachusetts, and author, most recently, of *Resource Wars: The New Landscape of Global Conflict* (Henry Holt / Metropolitan, 2001).

HARRY MAGDOFF is an editor of *Monthly Review*. The essays in this book honored his ninetieth birthday.

ROBERT W. MCCHESNEY was until recently an editor of *Monthly Review*. He is a professor at the Institute of Communications Research and the Graduate School of Information and Library science at the University of

Illinois at Urbana-Champaign. His most recent book is *The Problem of the Media: U.S. Communication Politics in the Twenty-First Century* (Monthly Review Press, 2004).

ELEANOR STEIN teaches telecommunications law at Albany Law School, and women and the law at the State University of New York at Albany.

WILLIAM K. TABB teaches economics at Queens College, City University of New York. He is the author of *The Amoral Elephant: Globalization and the Struggle for Social Justice in the Twenty- First Century* (Monthly Review Press, 2001) and *Unequal Partners: A Primer on Globalization* (New Press, 2002).

YANIS VAROUFAKIS teaches political economy at the University of Athens, Greece.

IMMANUEL WALLERSTEIN directs the Fernand Braudel Center for the Study of Economies, Historical Systems, and Civilizations, is editor of *Review*, and Senior Research Scholar at Yale University. He is the author of *The Decline of American Power: The U.S. in a Chaotic World* (New Press, 2003).

NOTES

PREFACE

1 http://jfklibrary.org./j061063.htm; V.D. Sokolovskii, *Soviet Military Strategy* (Englewood Cliffs, N.J.: Prentice-Hall, 1963), 149; originally published in the Soviet Union in 1962 under the title *Military Strategy*. In his speech Kennedy substituted ellipses in the main part of the quotation offered here. Here we quote from the same passage, replacing the ellipses with the actual text.

2 Ronald Steel, *Pax Americana* (New York: Viking Press, 1967), 16–17, 268, 336.

3 Chalmers Johnson, *The Sorrows of Empire: Militarism, Secrecy and the End of the Republic* (New York: Henry Holt, 2003), 1.

4 Ronald Steel, *Pax Americana* (New York: Viking Press, 1970), 334.

5 Harry Magdoff and Paul M. Sweezy, "Pox Americana," *Monthly Review*, 43: 3 (July–August 1991), 1–13.

CHAPTER 1

1 "Manifest Destiny Warmed Up?" *Economist*, August 14, 2003.

2 Jonathan Marcus, July 17, 2003, www.bbc.co.uk/specials/1020_ageofempire/index.shtml.

3 The following brief historical treatment of the Philippine–American War draws mainly on the these works: Henry F. Graff, ed., *American Imperialism and the Philippine Insurrection: Testimony Taken from Hearings on Affairs in the Philippine Islands before the Senate Committee on the Philippines—1902* (Boston: Little, Brown, 1969); Angel Velasco Shaw and Luis H. Francia, *Vestiges of War: The Philippine-American War and the Aftermath of an Imperial Dream, 1899–1999* (New York: New York University Press, 2002); Daniel B. Schirmer, *Republic or Empire: American Resistance to the Philippine War* (Cambridge, Mass.: Schenkman, 1972) and "How the Philippine-U.S. War Began," *Monthly Review*, September 1999; Stuart Creighton Miller, *"Benevolent Assimilation": The American Conquest of the Philippines, 1899–1903* (New Haven: Yale University Press, 1990); and Daniel B. Schirmer and Stephen Rosskamm Shalom, *The Philippines Reader* (Boston: South End Press, 1987).

4 The poem is often reproduced without the subtitle. For a correct version see *Kipling's Verse: Definitive Edition* (New York: Doubleday, 1940).

5 Although a quarter of a million is the "consensus" figure of historians, estimates of Fil-

ipino deaths from the war have ranged as high as one million, which would have meant depopulation of the islands by around one-sixth.

6 Jim Zwick, ed., *Mark Twain's Weapons of Satire* (Syracuse, N.Y.: Syracuse University Press, 1992), 172. For information on the Moro massacre and the W. E. B. DuBois quote see www.boondocksnet.com/ai/ail/moro.html. Jim Zwick's boondocksnet.com website is a crucial source for materials on the Philippine-American War, contemporary responses to Kipling's "White Man's Burden," and Mark Twain's anti-imperialist writings.

7 See www.boondocksnet.com/ai/ailtexts/mm_featarms.html. The Nobel committee was, however, mainly impressed by Kipling's sympathy for the Boers in South Africa—another population of white colonizers.

8 *Wall Street Journal*, July 15, 2003.

9 *New York Times Magazine*, September 7, 2003.

10 Max Boot, *The Savage Wars of Peace: Small Wars and the Rise of American Power* (New York: Basic Books, 2003).

11 *New York Times Magazine*, July 28, 2002.

12 Niall Ferguson, *Empire: The Rise and Demise of the British World Order and the Lessons for Global Power* (New York: Basic Books, 2003).

13 This call upon white elites to divide the world evoked a response beyond Britain and the United States. The admiration of Kipling among the ruling classes at the center of the capitalist world was more general. As Hobsbawm tells us: "When the writer Rudyard Kipling, the bard of the Indian empire, was believed to be dying of pneumonia in 1899, not only the British and the Americans grieved—Kipling had just addressed a poem on 'The White Man's Burden' to the USA on its responsibilities in the Philippines—but the Emperor of Germany sent a telegram." Eric Hobsbawm, *The Age of Empire* (New York: Vintage, 1987), 82.

CHAPTER 3

1 Peter Baker, "Wrong Turn in Nasiriyah Led to Soldiers' Capture; Maintenance Company Drove into Waiting Ambush," *Washington Post*, April 13, 2003.

2 Edward Said, "Give Us Back Our Democracy: Americans Have Been Cheated and Lied To," www.counterpunch.org, April 21, 2003.

3 Perry Miller, *Errand in the Wilderness* (Cambridge, Mass.: Harvard University Press, 1956), 114.

4 Henry Kamen, *The Spanish Inquisition* (New York: New American Library, 1965), 2.

5 Norman Roth, *Conversos, Inquisition, and the Expulsion of the Jews from Spain* (Madison: University of Wisconsin Press, 1995), 229.

6 David Stannard, *American Holocaust* (New York: Oxford University Press, 1992).

7 Kamen, *Inquisition*, 117–18.

8 Claudio Sánchez Albornoz, España*, un enigma histórico* (Buenos Aires, 1962), 1: 677.

9 Richard Slotkin, *Regeneration through Violence* (Middletown, Conn.: Wesleyan University Press, 1973), 42.

10 Francis Jennings, *The Invasion of America* (New York: W. W. Norton, 1975), 168.

11 L. Perry Curtis Jr., ed., *Apes and Angels* (Washington, D.C.: Smithsonian Institution, 1971).

12 Walter A. McDougall, *Promised Land, Crusader State* (New York: Houghton Mifflin, 1997), 95.

13 Samir Amin, *Empire of Chaos* (New York: Monthly Review Press, 1992), 9.

14 William Appleman Williams, *Empire as a Way of Life* (New York: Oxford University Press, 1980).

15 Warren Zimmerman, *First Great Triumph* (New York: Farrar Straus and Giroux, 2002), 17.

16 Howard Adams, *Prison of Grass* (Toronto: Free Press, 1974).

17 Harry Magdoff, Introduction to *Imperialism in the Seventies* by Pierre Jalée (New York: Monthly Review Press, 1973), xvii–xviii.

CHAPTER 5

1 Warren Zimmermann, *First Great Triumph* (New York: Farrar, Straus and Giroux, 2002).

2 Available at www.whitehouse.gov/nsc/nss.html.

3 For more on the emerging power struggle in the Caspian Sea basin, see my *Resource Wars: The New Landscape of Global Conflict* (New York: Henry Holt/Metropolitan, 2001).

CHAPTER 6

1 The pattern was somewhat different in Japan and East Asia, where the power of labor was much weaker, U.S. military-related demand during the Korean War was much stronger, and an export-oriented growth strategy directed at the U.S. market was much stronger.

2 The new (Anglo-) American capitalist model is typically presented in the language of economics and called monetarism or a free market deregulation approach or "neoliberal" economics. But it is as much about politics as economics: about freeing the state from its social commitments to the mass of citizens and using the state's powers much more narrowly to enhance the social power of capital. It is simultaneously a new way of expanding outwards in both politics and economics.

3 Peter Gowan, *The Global Gamble* (London: Verso, 1999).

4 Joanne Gowa, *Closing the Gold Window. Domestic Politics and the End of Bretton Woods* (Ithaca and London: Cornell University Press, 1983).

5 John Williamson, *The Failure of International Monetary Reform 1971–1974* (New York: New York University Press, 1977).

6 This is not to deny that there are objective limits to U.S. Treasury efforts, but these limits are wide. A useful discussion of the failings of mainstream economic explanations for

exchange rate swings can be found in Paul de Grauwe, *International Money* (Oxford: Oxford University Press, 1996).

7 Paul Wolfowitz has written persuasively about the emerging programmatic consensus. See Paul Wolfowitz, "Remembering the Future," *National Interest* 59 (Spring, 2000). The programmatic convergence between the Wolfowitz-Lewis Libby positions in the 1992 *Defense Planning Guidance* and the conceptions of the Clinton administration are evident in Clinton national security adviser Anthony Lake's key policy statements: see Anthony Lake "From Containment to Enlargement" (speech, School of Advanced International Studies, Johns Hopkins University, Washington, D.C., September 21, 1993) and Anthony Lake, "Laying the Foundation for a Post-Cold War World: National Security in the 21st Century"(speech, Chicago Council on Foreign Relations, May 24, 1996).

CHAPTER 7

1 Harry Magdoff, *Imperialism: From the Colonial Age to the Present* (New York: Monthly Review Press, 1979).

2 Henry A. Kissinger, *Years of Upheaval* (New York: Little Brown & Company, 1982).

3 Thomas Ferguson and Joel Rogers, *Right Turn: The Decline of the Democrats and the Future of American Politics* (New York: Hill & Wang Publishers, 1986), p. 97.

4 Richard Perle, "A Clean Break: A New Strategy for Securing the Realm," at www.israeleconomy.org/strat1.htm>.

5 Richard N. Haass, "Imperial America," Brookings Institution, 1999, at www.brook.edu/dybdocroot/views/articles/haass/19990909primary_FA.htm.

6 See <www.house.gov/international_relations/105th/ap/wsap212982.htm>.

CHAPTER 8

1 Peter Marcuse, "The Language of Globalization," *Monthly Review* 52 (July-August, 2000), 23.

2 Ibid.

3 Charles S. Maier, "An American Empire?" *Harvard Magazine*, November-December 2002.

4 Perry Anderson, "Force and Consent," *New Left Review* II: 17 (September-October 2002).

5 Samuel P. Huntington, "The Lonely Superpower," *Foreign Affairs*, March-April 1999.

CHAPTER 9

1 Emmanuel Todd, *After the Empire: The Breakdown of the American Order* (New York: Columbia University Press, 2004).

2 Ibid.

3 This article is adapted from *Al-Ahram Weekly Online* no. 627, February 27-March 5, 2003.

CHAPTER 10

1 Here I examine the possibility of anti-imperialist struggles from the perspective of the peoples of the third world. Yet, in the age of imperialism, all local struggles have an international dimension. The recovery of the dignity of labor as part of human freedom by workers of the first world is also an integral part of that struggle. Solidarity with genuine anti-imperialist movements across the globe is absolutely essential.

CHAPTER 12

1 Robert Brenner, *The Boom and the Bubble* (London: Verso, 2002).
2 For more detail on the critique of arguments indicating the continuation of the American economic crisis of the 70s through to today see Sam Gindin and Leo Panitch, "Rethinking Crisis," *Monthly Review* 54 (November, 2002). See also the response by the *Monthly Review* editors in the same issue.
3 N.icos Poulantzas, *Classes in Contemporary Capitalism* (London: NLB, 1974), 87. In this regard, note that the significance of the recent "confrontation" on Iraq between France, Germany, and Russia on the one hand and the United States on the other did not lie in the potentials for escalating division within the elite, but rather in the openings created by the public discord at the top for mobilization from below.
4 Cited by H. L. Robinson, "The Downfall of the Dollar" in R. Miliband and J. Saville, eds., *Socialist Register 1973* (London: Merlin Press, 1974), 417.
5 William White, "International Financial Crises: Prevention, Management and Resolution," March 20, 2003, bank for International Settlements, www.bis.org/speeches/sp0303020.htm.
6 Based on interviews by Leo Panitch and Sam Gindin with Paul Volcker and officials from the German Bundesbank and U.K. Treasury.
7 See Dick Bryan, *The Chase around the Globe* (Boulder, Colo.: Westview Press,1995).
8 Karl Marx and Friedrich Engels, *The Communist Manifesto* (London: Merlin, 2000), 11.

CHAPTER 14

1 Greg Robinson, *By Order of the President: FDR and the Internment of Japanese Americans* (Cambridge, Mass.: Harvard University Press, 2003).
2 See www.law.com/jsp/article.jsp?id=1052440755868.

CHAPTER 16

1 John Hobson, *Imperialism, A Study* (New York: James Pott and Co., 1902).
2 "The Shadow Men," *Economist*, April 24, 2003.
3 Harry Magdoff, *The Age of Imperialism: The Economics of U.S. Imperialism* (New York: Monthly Review Press, 1969), 1.
4 This argument was succinctly expressed in Paul Baran and Paul Sweezy's *Monopoly*

Capital: An Essay on the American Economic and Social Order (New York: Monthly Review Press, 1966), 183–202.

5 Magdoff, *The Age of Imperialism*, 16.

6 Robert W. Tucker, *The Radical Left and American Foreign Policy* (Baltimore, Md.: Johns Hopkins University Press, 1971), 28.

7 Ibid., 131.

8 Robert W. Tucker and David C. Hendrickson, *The Imperial Temptation: The New World Order and America's Purpose* (New York: Council on Foreign Relations Press, 1992), 14–15.

9 Ibid., 147.

10 Ibid., 10–11.

11 Richard N. Haass, *Intervention: The Use of American Military Force in the Post-Cold War World* (Washington, D.C.: Carnegie Endowment for International Peace, 1994), 8.

12 Richard N. Haass, *The Reluctant Sheriff: The United States after the Cold War* (New York: Council on Foreign Relations Press, 1998), 93.

13 *New York Times*, March 8, 1992.

14 Haass, *The Reluctant Sheriff*, 54.

15 Richard N. Haass, "Imperial America," Brookings Institution, 1999, www.brook.edu/dybdocroot/views/articles/haass/19990909primary_FA.htm. For a more detailed discussion of Haass's "Imperial America" argument, see John Bellamy Foster, "Imperial America and War," *Monthly Review* 55: 1 (May 2003).

16 Quoted in Michael Hirsh, *At War with Ourselves: Why America Is Squandering Its Chances to Build a Better World* (New York: Oxford University Press, 2003), 251.

17 Project for the New American Century, *Rebuilding America's Defenses: Strategy, Forces and Resources for a New Century* (Washington, D.C.: New American Century, 2000), http://www.newamericancentury.org/publictionsreports.htm.

18 For a treatment of how U.S. and NATO intervention in the Yugoslavian civil wars came to be seen in terms of a larger imperialist project see Diane Johnstone, *Fool's Crusade: Yugoslavia, NATO and Western Delusions* (New York: Monthly Review Press, 2002).

19 Max Boot, *The Savage Wars of Peace: Small Wars and the Rise of American Power* (New York: Basic Books, 2003).

20 This report is available at <http://www.whitehouse.gov/nsc/nss.html>.

21 Hirsh, *At War With Ourselves*, 245.

22 Ibid., 235.

23 Council on Foreign Relations, *Iraq, the Day After* (Washington, D.C.: Council on Foreign Relations, 2003), 48, http://www.cfr.org/publication.php?id=5681.

24 Project for the New American Century, *Rebuilding America's Defenses.*

25 Council on Foreign Relations, *Iraq, the Day After*, 48–49.

26 See Stephen Nathan, "The Prison Industry Goes Global," *Yes!*, Fall 2000, 34, www.futurenet.org/15prisons/nathan.htm.

27 István Mészáros, *Socialism or Barbarism* (New York: Monthly Review Press, 2001).A

INDEX